The Freshwater Angler™

ADVANCED
FLY FISHING

C. Boyd Pfeiffer

Creative Publishing
international

www.creativepub.com

C. BOYD PFEIFFER, an award-winning outdoor journalist and photographer, has been published in more than 70 magazines, including *Saltwater Fly Fishing, Outdoor Life,* and *American Angler.* He has authored 24 books on fishing and outdoor photography. He lives in Phoenix, Maryland.

To Brenda, who loves to fish

Creative Publishing international

Copyright © 2006 by Creative Publishing international, Inc.
18705 Lake Drive East
Chanhassen, MN 55317
1-800-328-3895
www.creativepub.com

President/CEO: Ken Fund

Executive Editor, Outdoor Group: Barbara Harold

Creative Director: Brad Springer

Book Designer: Kari Johnston

Production Manager: Laura Hokkanen

Printed in Singapore
10 9 8 7 6 5 4 3 2 1

ADVANCED FLY FISHING
by C. Boyd Pfeiffer

All Photos © C. Boyd Pfeiffer, except: pp. 4, 18, 19 (all), 23 (all), 38 (both), 39, 40 (both), 42 (all), 43 (all), 44 (all), 45, 47 (all), 50, 51 (both), 67, 68, 69 (both), 82 (both), 92 © Creative Publishing international, Inc.

Library of Congress Cataloging-in-Publication Data

Pfeiffer, C. Boyd.
  Advanced fly fishing : the complete how-to guide / C. Boyd Pfeiffer.
    p. cm. -- (Freshwater angler)
  Includes index.
  ISBN 1-58923-260-7 (hard cover)
  1. Fly fishing. I. Title. II. Series.
  SH456.P485 2006
  799.12'4--dc22   2005031739

ACKNOWLEDGMENTS

Those interested in a sport such as fly fishing start out by knowing that they know nothing, progress to the stage where they think that they know a little, and then get to the point where they know a lot, but also know that there is so much more to learn and so much that they do not know. I'm at that last stage.

Fortunately, fly fishing is a sport that can be practiced in so many ways, for so many different kinds of fish, on so many varieties of water, using so many special techniques and tactics. You never know them all, and you constantly learn nuances of the sport and methods of taking fish on the fly.

My learning has been with both strangers on foreign waters and with friends who put up with my various experiments with flies, tactics, methods and ideas on the sport. Fellow anglers such as Chuck Edghill, Lefty Kreh, Ed Russell, Norm Bartlett, Jim Heim, Bill May, Jack Goellner, Joe Zimmer, Vern Kirby and others have helped me over the years, more than they may ever realize. We have been friends longer than any of us would like to admit, and these friendships have been an anchor in my life. To all of them, I offer my thanks.

My thanks go especially to Joe Zimmer, a friend with whom I started fishing for bass on nearby lakes, then progressed to fishing with him in the Chesapeake Bay, with him then going on to concentrate on the rarified world of big-game fly fishing. While I have done some of this specialized fly sport, my thanks are to him for his advice and counsel on the world of big-game fly fishing, current tactics and special theories. Joe has caught—and released—hundreds of fly-caught billfish, including Atlantic and Pacific sailfish, white marlin and Atlantic blue marlin.

Thanks also to Dave Woronecki, a friend and retired biologist with the Maryland Department of Natural Resources who gave me additional insight and valued thoughts on releasing fish and the best ways to accomplish this. Bruce Richards also deserves mention for his ideas, knowledge and insights on fly lines that he has shared with me.

My thanks also to those many others—not strangers really—who, through meetings in fish camps, at club events, through fly fishing and fly tying clinics, at book signings, and other chance meetings in waders and boats, have (through comment, suggestion or question) added much to my thinking about fly fishing.

I give my thanks, also, to my editor, Barbara Harold, for her help, patience, advice and tolerance with my writing and schedule and to the staff at Creative Publishing International. My special thanks to my wife, Brenda, who put up with another hectic summer of writing and other tasks. Now, the kitchen is remodeled, the familyroom wood floor in place and the deck refinished. Let's go fly fishing for something!

Boyd Pfeiffer

ADVANCED FLY FISHING
TABLE OF CONTENTS

Introduction

You can't ever know it all, and no one person can corner the market on knowledge about every aspect of fly fishing, every fish, every body of water, every season and condition of the sport. Over the years, we all learn a lot, but over the years, we learn that there is still a lot to learn.

In a book like this, there is also the question of where to draw the line between basic information and advanced information, between the stuff that we all learn early and the stuff that is beyond the beginner books. How do we decide what is information that we all know and information that we all want to learn?

The answer is not easy, since the bare bones information on saltwater fly fishing might be just what is needed by an expert trout angler making his or her first foray into the salt and literally dipping a toe into the world of saltwater fly fishing. How to handle a little 3-weight rod and long leader might be totally new for someone who has spent a lifetime hoisting largemouth bass out of the grass with a fly rod and weedless bug.

This book is meant to give you an edge in all things fly fishing. It does not concentrate on the basics of knots, how to sharpen a hook, construction of fly lines, beginning fly casting methods, lists of fly patterns, where a trout lives or the seasonal movements of largemouth bass. It does attempt to show why some knots are better than others, why you don't need every fly rod made, how a floating saltwater line might—or might not—be right for your freshwater fishing, the pros and cons of direct drive versus anti-reverse reels, the advantages of reeling with your dominant hand, the right way to make a roll cast, considerations in fly choice for any fish, the best way to chum for saltwater fish, how to read any water, how to strike fish, how to fight big fish, proper fish-releasing tips and a lot more.

There are techniques of popping and swapping, swinging flies in the current for more strikes, casting under birds to avoid winged hook-ups, the count-down method to fly fishing, when to use a wide loop in casting, using sinking fly lines when weeds or grass are on top, fishing short leaders deep, fishing a floating fly with a sinking line and a sinking fly with a floating line. And more.

Read, enjoy and learn. Pass on what you learn from this book and your experiences on the water. Just don't forget to tell me your favorite tips when we meet someday on a stream, river, flat or bay.

Chapter 1

Rods, Reels, Lines

Tackle for smallmouth fishing like this can include anything that is heavy enough to turn over the line and throw the bugs. This 8-weight outfit was quite capable of taking this nice river smallmouth.

We all use fly tackle, but a lot of time that tackle and its use is misunderstood. It is also important to realize some oft-ignored basics when purchasing new tackle.

Simplify

By simplifying your tackle requirements, you can develop a tackle arsenal that has more choices for more effective approaches to all fly fishing. For example, you do not need one of each size rod/reel setup. Even without the big-game (15/19) outfit, that would be 13 rods (0-12). You can do quite nicely with 6 outfits.

Here are some considerations to keep in mind:

- Rods are designed to throw a specific weight line and fight fish of a certain weight/size. But modern rods have a lot of latitude in line weight and line length cast, to allow getting along without every rod size.
- With small lines, there is only a 20-grain (1.3-g) difference between two adjacent line sizes, up to a 6-weight. The difference increases in heavier lines but is no more than 50 grains (3.2 g) in the heaviest, excepting some big-game

lines in the 15/17 range.

- The difference between a 4-weight and 5-weight line is about 1/22 ounce (20 grains)—the 4-weight outfit using a line weighing 6/22 ounce (120 grains/7.8 g); the 5-weight outfit carrying a line weighing 7/22 ounce (140 grains/9 g). Even with heavy lines, the difference of 50 grains is less than 1/9 ounce.
- This difference in line weight is minimal and not enough to justify requiring every line/rod size if you don't already have them.
- Rod and line companies use line weight standards as guidelines, and line tolerances can make adjacent-size outfits very similar.

The alternate-size system reduces the number of separate lines/reels needed, saving money. Alternatively, you can get broader choices of line types (floating, sinking, sinking tip, tropical, cold weather, species-specific) for more variations with existing fly outfits. It also means that you can spend a few bucks on back-up reels/spools or rods. Getting every other rod/line size still gives you the breadth, with one or two extra rods/reels in each size to give you the depth of tackle for any trip.

With alternate line-size outfits, you can still cast the wide range of flies, from small bonefish to large tarpon. You can also use heavier or lighter lines on a given rod without serious difficulty by adjusting your casting.

Consider travel rods, preferably a four-piece style. These

are rarer in large sizes, but some companies now have rods in 10- through 12-foot (3- through 3.6-m) sizes in three- or four-piece models. Travel rods (three-, four-, five- or more-piece rods) work fine for local fishing; they also allow storage in short, large-diameter cases (such as an Abel travel rod case) to fit into a long duffle bag for easy travel.

When planning a new outfit, consider the order in which you buy equipment. Most anglers buy a rod, then a reel, then the fly line to fit it, then the leader and fly. I say that's wrong, since what you get might not be what you need. Buy tackle in the following order: fly, leader, line, reel and, finally, rod.

Consider the fish and what it eats or wants in fly design and size. You can handle small pike on a 6-weight outfit, but you can't cast the large pike flies. The fly—size and bulk—determines the leader and the line necessary to cast and turn over the fly.

After the fly, choose the

leader with the necessary tippet size and type (wire for barracuda, sharks and pike). Tippet size is important. Use a long leader for trout on crystal clear waters, but when you're deep fishing for pike or bass, use a short, 3-foot (0.9-m) leader on a sinking line.

Next, match the line to the fly and leader. A 4-weight line for bluegill can't turn over a 1/0 pike or barracuda fly. You can cast a size 14 trout fly with an 8-weight line, but it is overkill.

Then, get a reel that holds the line along with any necessary backing. You don't need backing for bluegill or white perch, but you might need it for pike—and you will definitely need it for big barracuda, stripers, bonefish, permit, bluefish, musky and similar large fish. Pick a reel to hold the line and backing.

Finally, pick the rod in the length needed to throw the line. That also means that for long casts—with any size line—

Most tackle for fly fishing is pretty simple. Tackle for big-game fly fishing requires heavy rods with fighting grips and large-capacity, anti-reverse reels such as these.

you want a long rod, preferably a 9-footer. You can get by with a very short rod if you are only going to make leader-and-a-few-feet-of-line casts for trout or if you just want to fool around with tiny rods for small-creek trout fishing.

Rods

From the standpoint of physics, there is no exception that the long rod—within reason—is best for casting. That means rods up to about 9 feet (2.7 m). Longer, and the rods become whippy, weak and casting suffers. The 9-foot rod is a long lever that allows for easier casting. This rod is best to get the fly to the fish. If you can't get the fly to the target area, you don't have a chance to fight a fish.

This does not mean that there is no place for short rods. The short, 6-foot (1.8-m) fly rods hyped forty years ago for the small limestone streams of southern Pennsylvania are still fine and fun for that type of fishing. There is also a place for any rod length provided that you are happy with and comfortable using it.

Long rods are best for poking through the brush to dap a fly into a small stream. They are also good for dapping in general, since the longer the rod, the easier you can follow a fly down a riffle to take trout. Long rods allow you to lift the line over limestone stream meadow grasses, or to keep the line out of the rigging when boat fishing. Short rods don't allow the reach to hold a fish away from a snaggy bank or out of some weeds, although short rods are best

for handling fish when casting from a boat.

For big game, 8½- to 9-foot (2.6- to 2.7-m) rods are best, but they must be tough and heavy. These rods—for everything from dolphin to billfish to sharks to tuna—must be a minimum of 12-weight, with some going to a 17- to 19-weight. The standard 8½- to 9-foot length allows casting the heavy line with only one backcast.

Rods must have good fittings. You need one guide for each foot (30.5 cm) or part of a foot of rod length. Guides must be sized properly (too large is better than too small). Large stripping guides are necessary to clear the line as it flows through the guides. On big-game fly rods, the rod must have large, size 6 snake guides above three stripping guides or have ceramic guides (aluminum

Most reel seats on freshwater rods (right) are designed to be attractive, such as these with wood inserts on trout and salmon rods (top three have inserts—bottom is all aluminum). The best of these will have double lock nuts. If an extension butt is added or incorporated into freshwater rods (second from the bottom) it should be short as shown here.

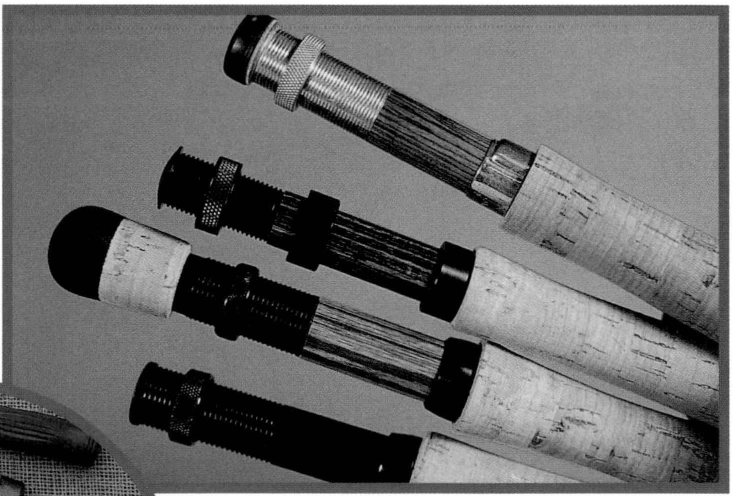

Many saltwater fly anglers like rods with an extension butt (left), although many also do not. It also helps to have a wide butt cap as on the top rod which makes it easier to rest the rod against you when fighting big fish. If used, extensions should be short to prevent line tangles. The bottom rod has a home-made extension designed to friction fit into the end of an aluminum reel seat.

oxide, aluminum nitride, SIC, other) throughout.

Rods must have a cork grip in a Wells or half-Wells shape, with the half-Wells put on properly—the swollen end toward the tip of the rod. This allows you to use your thumb on the grip to punch out a cast. (The reversed half-Wells or cigar grips make for a more attractive rod with the front taper of the grip, but are not as functional on rods over 6-weight. Form should follow function.) Big-game rods require a 6-inch (15.2-cm) "fighting grip" above the handle for leverage when lifting big fish.

Up-locking reel seats are best to provide a short extension from the butt end of the rod to the reel. This makes a *de facto* extension butt to keep the reel from tangling with clothing.

If possible—and a must with rods over 6-weight—make sure that the reel seat has two locking nuts to secure the sliding hood. Big rods (saltwater and big-game) must have solid reel seats (aluminum or graphite) rather than the attractive wood-insert reel seats found on trout rod models.

Saltwater rods benefit from having graphite and stainless hood Fuji-style reel seats that are not subject to corrosion problems as are aluminum seats.

If you do use a fighting (extension) butt or the rod comes with one, choose the shortest possible length. If you have to, cut it off to no more than 2 inches (5 cm) so that it does not tangle line when a fish runs and line coils jump off the boat deck to tangle around the butt.

The one exception with

Care of reels is important, particularly when fishing in saltwater where corrosion is always a problem. For best results, spray the reel with a demoisturizer such as WD-40 and rinse or soak the reel in fresh water after each day in saltwater fishing.

extension butts is with big-game rods, since with a one-cast-chance to get the fly to the fish, the line is out (hanging in the boat wash) when you make the cast, with little chance of it wrapping around the extension. Screw-in extensions are best—no more than 6 inches (15 cm), the maximum allowed by IGFA on big-game rods.

Reels

At one time, fly reels were thought of as storage places for fly line. We now realize that reels are a must—not only for holding the fly line and backing, but also for fighting fish.

Most reels are die cast, machined or die cast with some surfaces machined. This makes for a sturdy frame and spool that is better than the assembled reels of the past. Anodizing is vital. Type III hard anodizing in which protective chemicals penetrate the

aluminum to protect against corrosion is a must for saltwater reels. Reels with lighter anodizing or other finishes are okay for fresh water—not for salt water.

Drag

All reels have a drag, with the simplest being the click drag of a spring pawl riding against a gear-type wheel. Some of these are adjustable as to the tension in the spring. All are primarily found on freshwater reels.

Saltwater and big-fish reels must have a brake, which is how a drag functions. Drags vary from the simple pressure on a disc, to drum-type drags, to taper drags, to caliper drags (single or double). Disc drags work by the drag adjustment varying contact between the inner side of the spool and the disc (usually cork or synthetic—graphite in some cases) to create resistance when taking out line. Drum types work by adjusting the contact surfaces of the drum and braking sleeve, while taper drags work similarly using a tapered drum. Caliper drags work by caliper brake pads (one or two) contacting a turning wheel attached to the spool.

Of the various drag mechanisms, the cork disc drag is traditionally the most reliable. Cork is easily cleaned and also easily lubricated with neat's-foot oil.

Large Arbors

One of the big hypes today is with the "large-arbor" reels. Most of the so-called advantages are minimal. The justification is that large-arbor reels retrieve faster, reduce reeling fatigue, take in more line and do everything but slice bread. That's not true unless the overall reel diameter is larger than the replaced conventional reel.

If the overall diameter is not larger, then you are just fishing with a "reduced-line-capacity" reel, since the larger arbor is also reducing the amount of line (backing) that the reel holds.

The advantages of large-arbor reels are that if you have a reel with a 4-inch (10-cm) overall diameter, you retrieve about 12$\frac{1}{2}$ inches (32 cm) of line with each turn of the reel handle. With a 4$\frac{1}{2}$-inch-diameter (11.4-cm) reel, you retrieve about 14$\frac{1}{7}$ inches of line per handle turn. (Pi is 3.1416. Circumference of a circle is Pi times the diameter.)

Any purported advantage is slight—about 1$\frac{1}{2}$ inches (3.8 cm) of line per turn of the handle in this case. Large-arbor/diameter reels may hold less backing than the conventional reel. For big fish, assuming other factors to be equal, buy a large diameter conven-

The larger so-called arbor reels (left) do not necessarily hold any more backing and line than a conventional reel (right). The advantage of the larger arbor reel is often minimal and must be large enough and with enough backing capacity to make it truly an advantage in reeling in line, fast retrieve, etc.

tional reel to give you the slight reeling advantage along with greater line capacity. The only negative is the slight added weight and increased cost of any additional backing.

Direct-Drive Versus Anti-Reverse

Direct-drive reels have the handle attached to the spool. Anti-reverse reels have the handle attached to a plate or rim that is separate from the spool. On direct-drive reels, the handle turns as a fish runs against the drag. On a fast run, you can get a hard rap on the knuckles from the handle. With big-game reels, you can get a broken finger.

On anti-reverse reels, the handle does not turn as a fish takes line. Using an anti-reverse reel with light tackle and tippets (which must have a lightly-set drag), you can turn the handle easily without taking in line. They don't work well in these situations. Direct-drive reels are generally less expensive than anti-reverse reels (fewer parts, less construction).

The advantage of anti-reverse reels is when fishing for big fish with heavy leader tippets. Then you can feel the resistance as you reel against the drag. The other big advantage is that the handle does not become a weapon as it spins when a sailfish heads for the horizon at 60 miles per hour (96.5 kmph).

Big-game reels are usually best in anti-reverse models, built solid to take the abuse and strain when the other end of the line is attached to a 100-pound-plus (45-kg) marlin or Pacific sailfish. They must also have enough capacity for 400 to 600 yards (385 to 549 m) of 30-pound-test (13.6-kg) Dacron. Most reels have indications that suggest size of line and backing, or the preferred species of fish for that reel size.

Right-Hand Versus Left-Hand Reeling

Many anglers anguish as to whether they should reel right-handed or left-handed. Most experts, including Lefty Kreh, Mark Sosin, Stu Apte and others, believe that it is easier—and better—to switch hands (right to left) when reeling, to hold the rod with the left hand when fighting a fish and to use your right hand when cranking the reel. That, and the following, assumes a right-handed caster.

- Fly anglers who use spinning reels do not switch hands. They cast with the right hand and reel with the left. This is possible because the larger circles circumscribed by the longer spinning reel handles are less hard on the non-dominant hand and forearm.
- Fly anglers who use bait-casting tackle seldom use left-hand reels to cast with the right hand and reel with the left. They switch hands with each cast.
- Some anglers strongly disagree with the above, and continue to reel even big game catches with their non-dominant hand. That's fine—do what works best for you—but if your non-dominant hand gets tired or weak from reeling, consider the above.

Lines

Modern lines have a plastic coating on a braided or mono core. All types of lines—floating, shooting head, sinking, sinking tip, and others—are possible with this construction. The best line for most fishing is a weight-forward taper in one of many styles. Anglers argue that you can reverse a double-taper line end-to-end for more life from the line and that double tapers turn over more gently to present a fly slightly better for trout fishing. The first of these statements is true—but you must remember to reverse your line.

The second argument usually is not true. Presentation of a fly is mostly a function of the length of the front taper in terms of how it turns over and how gently it lands on the water. With the exception of a few "bass-bug tapers," the front taper of weight forward lines is usually as long, or even slightly longer, than similar double tapers made by the same

company. With the weight of the line in the belly, these can also be cast farther than double tapers. The big advantage of double tapers is that they make it easier to mend line and roll cast.

Floating

Today, weight-forward line varieties are often based on species. We have tarpon, bonefish, bass, trout, striper and other lines, all specifically designed for certain kinds of fishing or fish.

A check of line specifications of one manufacturer shows that the front taper, belly and back taper of three lines (freshwater bass, general saltwater and tropical bonefish) are identical for the same weight line. A tarpon line in a larger size (there is no overlap of line sizes for a direct comparison), is within 6 inches (15 cm) in specs of the above lines. (Tarpon and bonefish lines are of a stiffer formulation for tropical fishing and thus different in this regard.)

There are some differences.

Fly lines come in a variety of different colors. Often a bright fly line is best for big water and ocean fishing so that you can see the direction of the line and hooked fish. Clear or smoke is best when sight fishing to skinny water fish such as bonefish or trout.

For example, salt water is more buoyant than fresh water (on average, salt water is 1.03 and fresh water is 1.00). As a result, you can make floating lines for saltwater fishing a little denser (thinner for the weight) and they will still float as well as slightly thicker freshwater lines. This can aid casting, since thinner line of the same weight creates a different mass/air resistance ratio that allows casting farther, easier and with tighter loops than a slightly thicker line. If this is not that important to you, then you can use your freshwater floating line for saltwater fly fishing.

If you do use your saltwater floating line in fresh water, you might find that the line does not float as well or even becomes a very slow sinking line. Don't use your saltwater line when trout fishing dry flies, since the line might even sink slightly. A saltwater floating line in fresh water is great when fishing for bass or pike, where flotation is less important. The thinner, denser line casts better than a similar freshwater line and turns over large bass/pike flies easier.

Shooting Head

Shooting heads started out as sinking lines cobbled together by West Coast steelhead and salmon fly anglers, but today both floating and sinking models are available.

Some anglers use lead-core trolling lines cut into 30-foot (9-m) shooting heads. (Lead in some fishing tackle is restricted or illegal in an increasing number of fishing waters, states and Canadian provinces. Check before you fish. Non-lead lines are also available.) Both lead and non-lead are fine for making mini lead heads of a few feet (few meters) long rigged between the line and the leader.

Sinking and Sinking Tip

Sinking lines make it possible to sink flies to spots that previously never saw a fly and to fish where 95 percent of fish suck up 95 percent of their food. These lines include a sinking substance, such as tungsten, added to the plastic coating. The main advantage with these is that you can keep a fly in the strike zone longer—throughout the length of the cast after initially allowing the fly to sink. The disadvantage is that you have to retrieve almost all of the line and pick it up with an aerial roll cast—pulling it up and out of the water, rather than off the water.

Sinking-tip lines allow fishing deep with a line in which the fishing end sinks and the rest

Sink Rates

Sink Rate Number	Sink Rate Per Second
1	1/2 to 1 1/2 inch (1.3 to 3.8 cm)
2	1 1/2 to 2 1/2 inches (3.8 to 6.4 cm)
3	2 1/2 to 3 1/2 inches (6.4 to 8.9 cm)
4	3 1/2 to 4 1/2 inches (8.9 to 11.4 cm)
5	4 1/2 to 5 1/2 inches (11.4 to 14 cm)
6	5 1/2 to 6 1/2 inches (14 to 16.5 cm)
7	6 1/2 to 7 1/2 inches (16.5 to 19.1 cm)
8	7 1/2 to 8 1/2 inches (19.1 to 21.6 cm)
9	8 1/2 to 9 1/2 inches (21.6 to 24.1 cm)
10	9 1/2 to 10 1/2 inches (24.1 to 26.7 cm)

of the line floats. This makes for an easier pick-up, provided that the sinking end is not too long and that you can plane the line up on retrieve before casting. Consider the following with sinking tip lines:

- Sinking tip lines vary with the manufacturer as to sink rate and length of the sinking end, which varies from 5 to 35 feet (1.5 to 10.7 m).
- Lines with longer sinking tips get deeper but make pick-ups more difficult.
- With a very long sinking tip end, treat the line like a sinking line. Retrieve most of the line, then pull it out of the water to make an aerial roll cast for the next cast.
- Different sink rates are available with sinking and sinking-tip lines. New proposed standards use a number system for the sink rate rather than the old and confusing terminology of "slow sinking," "medium sinking" and "fast sinking."
- The new system will rate sinking and sinking tip lines as in the chart on page 12.

Marking Lines

Mark lines by their weight and sink rate. Mark the end of the line with the weight and mark the sink rate (on sinking lines) about 1 foot (30.5 cm) back. Use a black, permanent felt-tip marker on light colored floating lines and bright-colored nozzle-cap (for easy application) fabric paint on dark or sinking lines. Use a system with a wide line for a "5" and a narrow line for a "1." Thus, four narrow lines indicate a 4-weight line; 1 wide line and three narrow lines indicate an 8-weight, and so on.

Tackle for pike must include a rod and line heavy enough to turn over the big flies that are used to take big freshwater fish.

Color

Lines come in clear or colored. Clear, smoke or any pale sky color is best when fishing skinny water where fish might otherwise flare off, spooked by line in the air.

Cold-weather (for trout, steelhead—even if not labeled "cold water") and warm-weather lines (such as tropical lines) each have a different coating formulation to make the line flexible for cold weather or stiffer for warm weather. This provides consistency of handling that makes it easy to get out a cast and handle the line in any situation.

The short front taper and more rapid, forceful turnover of a bass-bug taper is a better choice than a general weight-forward line (longer front taper) when bass fishing with large flies and bugs.

When fishing for clear-water trout or tropical species, use a clear or smoke-colored line that is less visible in the air and less likely to spook fish.

For long casts, try a shooting head of about 30 feet (9 m) connected to a 100-foot (30.5-m) running line to give you a 130-foot (39.6-m) line in front of the Dacron backing.

For more line storage on any reel, consider chopping back the rear of a weight-forward line for added backing space. Do this too much, however, and you only chop back an expensive weight forward to make a shooting head that is lacking the running line.

One way to mark fly lines is to use felt tip makers to mark the line with wide or narrow bands to indicate a "5" or "1," using these marks in combination to indicate the weight of the fly line.

Chapter 2

Leaders, Waders, Vests, Fly Boxes

With experience, every fly angler accumulates a variety of additional equipment and accessories. Here are some items you may find useful.

Leaders

Leaders are a must as a connection between the line and the fly. When building your own leaders, use a simple formula of 50/30/20. This means that you make 50 percent of the leader the butt section, 30 percent the tapered portion and 20 percent the tippet.

An approximate guide to the tippet "X" system and pound-test measurement is to subtract the "X" number from 8 or 9 (line test varies with the brand) to get the pound-test. Thus, a 3X tippet is about 5- to 6-pound-test (2.2- to 2.7-kg); a 6X tippet about 2- to 3-pound-test (0.91- to 1.4-kg).

Use all the same brand of nylon mono for tying leaders to prevent a hinge, stiff section or odd color in the middle of a leader.

Use braided wire for pike and other toothy fish, attached with an Albright knot to a heavy mono tippet (15- to 20-pound-test/6.8- to 9-kg). Use a figure-eight knot to attach the fly for easy changes. Note that this "knot" only works with braided wire.

Waders or hip boots? Make your choice depending on the kind of fishing you will do and the depth of the water.

If you like fluorocarbon, use it for the tippet only. The fish won't care what you use at the other end of the leader. Never use fluorocarbon for fishing dry flies or even light surface bugs. The heavier material and fast sink rate of fluorocarbon may sink the fly.

Length

Leaders range from as short as 3 feet (0.9 m) for sinking lines and flies to about 15 feet (4.6 m) for delicate fly presentations. Most leaders are best at about 9 to 10 feet (2.7 to 3 m) long, with bass leaders best at about 6 to 7 1/2 feet (2 to 2.3 m) for easier turnover of air resistant bugs.

You can adjust this leader formula. For a lighter, slower presentation of the fly, use a long tippet section. For a fly or bug that does not turn over easily or falls back on the leader tippet, shorten the leader (butt or mid-section) to create a faster taper and quicker turnover of the fly.

Use very short leaders with sinking or sinking tip lines to keep the fly from suspending and fishing high in the water column. A 2-foot (60-cm) tippet and a 1-foot (30-cm) "butt" section one size larger than the tippet works fine, looped to the line. An alternative is to use the series of sinking leaders that are now available. These come in varying sink rates and various lengths, to which you attach the desired mono tippet.

If you want to lengthen a leader, replace the tippet with a much longer section or add the same diameter to the tippet end. Do this for spooky species

such as trout, bonefish and permit. Any excess slack in the tippet when casting creates more advantage than disadvantage by providing more action or natural drift to the fly.

Shorten leaders and their taper for turning over bulky flies and bass bugs. Lengthen the tippet section for spooky fish, such as clear-water trout and bonefish.

Knots

Big-game leaders can be bought, but are not widely sold. All other leader types can be bought from fly shops and catalogs. Even with a store-bought leader, you must add additional tippet material in time.

Whatever knot you are tying, use saliva as a lubricant to prevent friction and heat build up. When tying knots to connect sections, clip the ends close after pulling the knot tight.

It pays to learn a few good knots. Here are the ones I suggest:

- The improved clinch knot. This is not rated as strong as the Palomar, but it is easier to tie. The Palomar requires a loop that is brought over the fly or lure and thus is easier to mix up or get tangled on large flies or those with tandem hooks.
- The Palomar knot. This knot is rated slightly stronger than the improved clinch knot, but is more complicated to tie.
- The blood knot. This simple knot joins two strands of mono. Provided that the two lengths are not widely dissimilar in diameter, the knot pulls up easily. If there is a wide disparity of diameter in the two strands, make five

One special knot that works only for braided wire when fishing for toothy fish such as pike, bluefish, and barracuda is the figure-eight knot that can be backed out of a fly eye for easy, instant change of flies.

turns (standard) with the thinner mono and three to four turns with the thicker end. This pulls up easier and is still as strong as a conventional knot.

- A good loop knot. Pick the perfection loop, surgeon's loop or the figure-eight loop. Of these, the perfection loop is easiest to tie in small mono diameters; the surgeon's loop best in heavier mono butt sections (40- to 50-pound-test/18.1- to 22.7-kg).

  Use a loop knot in the butt end of the leader for easy interchangeable loop-to-loop line connections. Use a butt loop or folded fly line loop in the end of your fly line for this connection.

- The nail knot. This is often used to connect the leader to the fly line. Done right, it is a good strong knot, although it does not allow the versatility of loop-to-loop connections.

  If you do not like interconnecting loops, use a nail knot coated with Pliobond.

- Braided wire figure-eight knot. This is a knot that only works in braided (twisted) wire. It is ideal for toothy fish. It allows you to back out the wire to remove the fly and to "tie" on a new fly. It is a simple, effective knot, but for braided wire only.

If you are venturing into tropical salt water or big-game fishing, there are some other knots that you need to know. These include:

- The Bimini twist. This is a 100-percent loop knot. You can tie it in braid (Dacron, gel spun), monofilament nylon or fluorocarbon. Practice this knot first and tie up any needed loops before leaving the dock. It is difficult to tie on a rocking boat.
- The spider hitch. This is easier to tie than the Bimini and rated a 100-percent knot. It is not as good as the Bimini, however, and can fail if not pulled up carefully.
- The Homer Rhode loop knot. This easy knot provides a loop in the heavy tippet (bite or shock section of 50- to 100-pound-test/22.7- to 45.4-kg) tied to the fly. It is not a strong knot, which does not matter when using heavy shock material. Even with significant strength loss, it is still stronger than the tippet. This knot allows for maximum fly movement.
- The Albright. This is the best knot for tying a light leader to a very heavy shock section. It is strongest when you tie the light line in a Bimini and then use the two strands to tie close and tight to the folded loop made in the heavy shock section.

The Fluorocarbon Option

The big interest at this writing is fluorocarbon leader material. If you like it, that's fine. But only use it for the tippet. When mixing it with mono, make both the mono nylon and fluorocarbon the same color. Here is some information about fluorocarbon:

- In comparison to mono, manufacturers claim that fluorocarbon is less visible, has a faster sink rate, has better abrasion resistance and has no water absorption.
- Against this is that the decreased visibility is slight (1.33 refractive index of water, 1.52 of mono and 1.42 of fluorocarbon).
- Fluorocarbon also has a specific gravity of 1.76 to the nylon mono of 1.14 (water is 1.0). If you are fishing with a full fluorocarbon leader attached to a light (1- to 4-weight) line, the entire leader sinks, making your outfit into a *de facto* sinking tip. Don't use this for dry fly or sub-surface trout fishing.
- You might argue that fluorocarbon is good for short leaders on sinking and sinking tip lines, although then the visibility factor is less important.
- Fluorocarbon is stiffer than mono, reducing any action in the fly.
- Some brands of fluorocarbon have a decreased tensile strength, so that you might have to use a heavier (read thicker) section to make up for that loss in strength, thus reducing some of the "less visible" advantage.
- The same thing applies to the reduced knot strength when compared to mono—knots in fluorocarbon are weaker.
- Fluorocarbon is more environmentally damaging than nylon, as fluorocarbon breaks down more slowly.
- Fluorocarbon is more expensive than premium mono.

Leader Tips for Billfish

Most big-game leaders are about 8 feet (2.4 m) in length, both for casting ease and also easy turnover of the big flies used. Use a loop-to-loop connection system for interchangeability of parts and flies. Big-game leaders also include a shock leader (bite section), and if you are fishing for record or in a fly tournament, you must adhere to International Game Fish Association regulations. Start with a 50-pound-test (22.7-kg) butt and continue to a 20-pound/9-kg (maximum, if fishing to IGFA rules) tippet and perhaps a 50- to 100-pound-test (22.7- to 45.4-kg) shock (or bite) leader.

Here are a few tips on rigging big-game line/leaders for billfish:

- Start with a loop-to-loop system in all of your tackle—backing to running line, to shooting head (or weight forward line if not using running line/shooting head system), to leader butt section, to IGFA leader section.
- These loops vary with the line section on which you are working. Use a spliced loop (done in Dacron with a splicing needle) or a Bimini twist for the backing loop. Make this loop large so that you can pass the reel through it when making connections.
- Use a folded and whipped fly-line loop or handmade or preformed braided loop on both ends of the running line on shooting heads.

If using some other running line (mono or braided mono), use an appropriate loop. For mono running lines, use a loop knot such as a surgeon's loop knot. For a braided running line, fold and whip as you do a fly line, and then seal with Pliobond.

- For the fly line or shooting head, use a folded and whipped fly line loop, a preformed braided loop or a hand-tied braided loop. Tie a loop knot (perfection loop, surgeon's loop or figure-eight loop) to both ends of the butt section of the leader. To the IGFA leader section tie in a Bimini and then tie a short surgeon's loop knot for attachment to the butt leader section. On the other end (tippet), tie in a Bimini and then tie a standard surgeon's knot or Albright to the heavy shock/bite section.
- Use a Homer Rhode knot or crimped leader sleeve to secure the fly to the 50- to 100-pound (22.7- to 45.4-kg) mono shock section.
- To make a simple shooting head and running line system, buy full length weight forward sinking billfish/big-game lines, and cut them in back of the rear taper. Use the tapered section to make your shooting head (about 30 to 35 feet/9.1 to 10.7 m) and the rear length (about 60 to 70 feet/18.3 to 21.3 m) for the running line. The advantage of this over the full weight forward line is that you can easily change shooting heads without changing the full fly line or switch between the shooting head/running line and a full weight forward line system.
- If using braided loops or making your own to attach a loop to a fly line, use Pliobond as a sealer. It has greater penetration than other flexible sealers, and glues to the line better. Do not use inflexible cements.

Waders

There are lots of choices when it comes to waders and hip boots for fly fishing. Waders and hip boots allow you to wade in different water depths. Consider hip boots if wading only shallow streams. Consider waders if wading mostly deep water.

Both come in boot-foot or stocking-foot style. The stocking-foot style is for use with separate wading boots. The boot-foot style are easy to use and travel with (no extra boots or gravel guard). If you have bad ankles or feet, the stocking-foot style with separate fitted boot provides more support.

If you are going to wear waders with a float tube, use stocking-foot waders that you can fit into swim fins.

To avoid getting several different pairs of waders, buy thin travel-style lightweight waders. Insulate these for cold water fishing with flannel pajama bottoms or sweat pants under your regular pants. If you are only wading cold waters for steelhead and salmon, use insulated or neoprene waders.

If you are a guide or fishing dozens of days per year, get expensive better waders for longer wader life. Otherwise, get inexpensive waders, since most material can disintegrate before you wear it out. If you kneel a lot (as you should when fishing small streams) buy knee pads to protect your waders.

For safety, always use a belt on the outside of your waders to reduce water intake should you fall in.

Nylon is economical, lightweight and comfortable in hot weather. Wear fleece or wool pants for added insulation when you're wading in cold water.

Rubber (left) is inexpensive and durable, but can be heavy and baggy. Most rubber waders are not suited for wading in very warm or cold weather.

Breathable (bottom left) materials, such as Gore-Tex, weigh about the same as nylon but are cooler in temperate water.

Neoprene (bottom right) is warm, comfortable and durable, and it provides some floatation if you fall in. Neoprene wading gear is available in several thicknesses, ranging from 3 mm to 5 mm. It lets you move more easily than rubber or nylon, and fits tighter for less water resistance in swift current. But neoprene is more expensive than other materials and may be too warm in hot weather.

Vests are a handy adjunct for the fly angler, since they serve the same purpose as a tackle box for boat anglers.

Here, Randy Vance holds a nice Missouri trout caught using one of the many flies that he carries in his many-pocket fishing vest.

Fishing Vest

Fishing vests are really nothing more than pockets sewn together to hold fly-fishing gear. Here are some considerations for choosing a vest.

Long vests hold more gear, while short vests are best for deep wading. If you fish mostly during hot weather, get a cooler mesh-style vest.

Most vests have zipper or hook-and-loop pocket fasteners. Pick the type of closure that you like. Zippers are surer closures, but sometimes require two hands to operate.

If you carry a net, make sure that the vest has a D-ring on the back neck for net attachment. The most comfortable vests have a soft knitted or yoke-style neck to prevent strain.

Pick a vest with pockets that are suitable for your fishing. Some can have up to 30-plus pockets. You don't need that many if you fish with only a few fly boxes and have simple gear requirements. Make sure that the vest has pockets to hold the size fly boxes you have.

Some vests have specialty pockets for sunglasses, stream thermometers, tippet spools, hemostats, pliers and other tools. Consider these vests if

you use these tools and like this pocket arrangement. Some vests have multiple rear pockets that are ideal for lunch, water bottles, spare reels/ spools and rain gear for long day trips.

Pick a vest color appropriate for your fishing. Light tan or blue is best for fishing in open areas; camouflage or green is best for wooded trout fishing.

If using only one or two fly boxes (such as for saltwater wading or bass fishing) consider a small shoulder pack instead of a vest. These easily hold a fly box or two, nippers and a leader tippet spool. They are light and comfortable.

Fly Boxes

Fly containers are vital to fly fishing. Most of us carry anywhere from a few dozen to a few hundred flies. Fly boxes come in a variety of styles, but over the years, I have simplified to just a few styles, depending upon the outing.

Slit-Foam

Scientific Anglers and C&F Design are the only manufacturers of slit-foam boxes. Sliced open cell foam (called micro-slit-foam) tightly holds a fly hook in the slit between the two sides of foam. They are available for small and large flies, with one box featuring slits for 470 flies while other boxes are spaced for fewer large warmwater and saltwater flies.

Compartment

DeWitt boxes were the original lightweight compartment boxes and are still great. They are very lightweight, although not as sturdy as the "lure-style" boxes available. I like these in the square compartment style for trout dry flies and for bulky flies such as crabs for permit, hellgrammites for smallmouth and large nymphs for trout.

Lure boxes with long compartments (cross-wise or length-wise in the box) for larger flies are also good. These are ideal for barracuda flies, tarpon flies, large Deceivers, Quick minnows, bass bugs, saltwater poppers and Clousers. These are of a heavier plastic than the DeWitt style boxes, but they are typically carried in a boat or with only one box used for some wade fishing.

Clip-Style

Perrine-style aluminum boxes have coil springs or clips to hold flies. Different size clips are available in different boxes. I like the larger clips for salmon (Atlantic and Pacific), shad, steelhead and similar flies.

Soft Binders

Soft notebook-style cases are sold in general tackle shops for holding spinnerbaits, buzzbaits, jigs and soft plastics. These are ideal for large saltwater and warmwater flies. Most come with zipper-style plastic bags, but I like the cloth/clear-face zippered notebook style pencil cases sold in general and school supply stores. These come in many colors to color code your fly storage. Soft lure containers include pockets for storage of wire leader coils (pike, musky, bluefish and barracuda), fluorocarbon (trout and bonefish), mini lead heads (for sinking leaders and flies), nippers or other leader/fly necessities. Handles make them easy to carry for boat use.

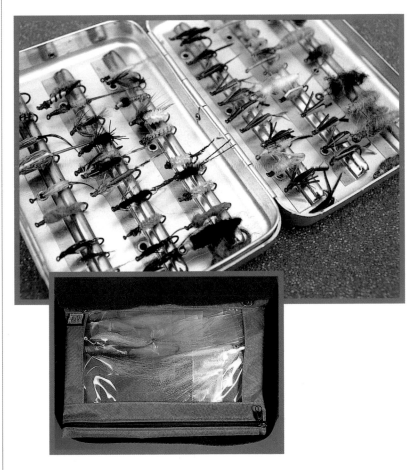

Flies are best organized in fly boxes (top) by type, with this box of nymphs suitable for most eastern trout fishing. It helps to have boxes separated into basic fly categories for easy selection on the stream.

One way to easily hold and carry large flies on a boat is to make and use a notebook carrier (bottom), such as this spinnerbait holder that has been rigged with clear pencil cases to hold flies. Different colors are available to color code your flies if desired.

Miscellaneous

In addition to the previous basics (flies are discussed in Chapter 3) consider the following:

- Cap—Wear a brimmed or ball-style cap with a dark underbrim to reduce glare from bouncing off the water, the underbrim and into your eyes. The result is less eye strain and easier spotting of fish.
- Sunglasses—Use only polarizing sunglasses. The wraparound type for side protection is best. Large lenses are also good for eye protection from glare and miss-cast flies. Use dark glasses (dark brown or gray) for bright sun conditions. Most of these have a transmission of 12 to 15 percent. For low light levels, use light tan or yellow glasses, with the yellow creating more contrast and better vision under subdued light. These usually have a transmission of about 25 to 35 percent. To help reduce glare and increase your ability to see beneath the water, tilt your head slightly from side to side.
- Sunscreen—Sunscreen is a must. Use it on any uncovered body part—your hands, face and head. Spread it with the back of your hand to avoid getting it on your palms and then onto flies where the smell might spook the fish. Use a waterproof brand with an SPF of 30 or more.
- Leader nippers—The best leader nippers are those that are like fingernail clippers without the lever arm—just squeeze to cut leader tippets. If you use fingernail clippers, remove the lever arm.
- Pliers—Pliers are necessary for some fly fishing, primarily when after large fish. You'll also need them to bend down barbs on warmwater and saltwater flies. Carry pliers belted in a sheath or, when boat fishing, loose in a bag.
- Net—Your fishing life will be simpler if you can land and handle fish without a net. (See Chapter 9 for more information.)
- Spare leader and tippet spools—Carry a few made-up leaders (store-bought or home tied) and carry extra spools of leader material for field repairs.
- Mini lead heads for sinking leaders—Make these from lead or non-lead trolling line or buy them ready made from Gudebrod, Orvis, Cortland and others. They are short looped-end lengths of sinking line added between a line and leader that help you get a fly down. Commercially, they come in 3- to 5-foot (0.9- to 1.5-m) lengths, but I make mine in 2-foot (0.6-m) lengths with looped ends for single or tandem use.
- Leader sink—These are sold to sink leaders, which tend to float sometimes until they absorb water. River bank mud is a good substitute.
- Dry fly floatant—This is designed to float flies by keeping them waterproof. Many brands are available.
- Amadou—This (or the synthetic patches) is good to blot the water and fish slime off your dry flies for better floatation.
- Line cleaner—It is best to use line cleaner before or after each fishing trip, but carry some just in case your line needs a little extra flotation treatment during a lunch break.
- Clip-on flashlight—If you fish at dawn, at dusk or

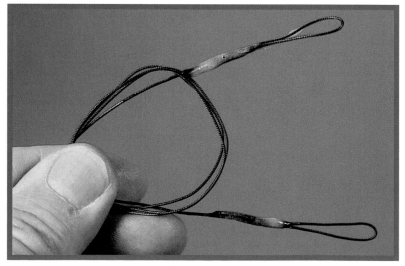

Mini lead heads like this, which was made by the author, can also be bought from companies such as Gudebrod, Orvis and Cortland. These ensure keeping a fly down in the water column with the fish when using sinking or sinking tip lines and allow you to "make" a temporary sinking tip line from your floating line using loop-to-loop connectors.

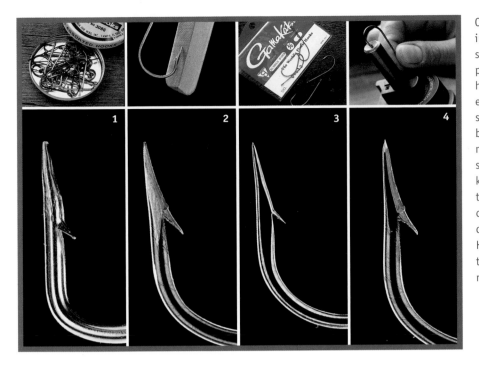

Ordinary hooks are surprisingly dull (1). You can sharpen them to a triangular point with a file or hook hone (2). Chemically sharpened hooks (3) are even sharper than filed hooks, but they cost up to 10 times more. A good motorized sharpener (4) makes the keenest point of all, though they're a bit too bulky to carry if you fish on foot. One of the best is the Pointmatic Hook-Hone-R, which is easy to use and has long-lasting rechargeable batteries.

during heavily overcast days, a small clip-on flashlight helps when threading a tippet through the fly eye. These are available for clipping to a vest pocket or cap.

- Rain parka—Carry a small disposable plastic rain parka. It folds to cigarette pack size and costs about a buck. Use it as long as possible and then recycle it with plastics.
- Fingerless gloves—For cold weather fishing, these are a must to stay comfortable, yet still be able to tie on flies and handle gear.
- Hook/fly releaser (for more information, see Chapter 9).
- Hook hone or diamond file— I like those from Diamond Machining Technology, but many brands are available. In a pinch, use a diamond fingernail file available for a few bucks from a drug or variety store.
- Snacks and water bottle— Some (hypoglycemic) anglers

get low blood sugar and need a power boost in the afternoon. Carry what you need—with water a must for all of us, particularly on hot days.

- Small camera—Many tiny cameras, both film and digital, are available to take hero shots of your catch and those of your friends. Carry in a zipper-sealed plastic sandwich bag in a fastened (button, Velcro or zipper) vest or shirt pocket. You must fasten the pocket or you may lose the camera!
- Strike indicators—Of the many types of indicators, the best are those of unprocessed wool yarn with black and fluorescent colors the most visible.
- Split shot or lead wire— Lead or non-lead products are sometimes necessary to get a fly deep—an assortment pack of various sizes of split shot or twist-on wire is a must. If you use the

shiny twist-on lead sheets, dull them first at home with vinegar.

- Stream thermometer—While thought of primarily for trout fishing, a stream thermometer gives you the water temperature and allows you to adjust your fishing accordingly. Colder than typical water temperatures require slow fishing, while warm temperatures require fishing deep in the cooler part of the water column. One tip is to use the electronic thermometers that allow you to hang a probe in the water to check for ambient air or water temperature at any time. You can use these while wading or boat fishing.

Chapter 3

Choosing the Right Fly

Flies come in both imitative and attractor styles. These, displayed in a Canadian fly shop, are examples of the right color attractor styles that are used for explorer fishing and to locate fish when blind casting.

Flies are often designed for a particular species. The term "trout flies" brings forth a concept of small flies designed to imitate various insects. You have dry flies, wet flies, nymphs, terrestrials, streamers and some that fall into a miscellaneous category. The same applies to flies you tie for bass, steelhead, Pacific salmon, Atlantic salmon, shad, pike and (sometimes) carp. In saltwater, some flies are specific for bluefish, bonefish, tarpon, snook, big game (marlin, sails and dolphin), stripers, redfish, barracuda and others.

We also have generic flies that can fit a number of species. Some, such as the Muddler minnow, were designed for trout, but are also excellent for smallmouth and largemouth bass. Lefty's Deceiver, designed by Lefty Kreh for Chesapeake Bay stripers, is a generic design that has taken dozens of fresh- and

Mayflies, such as these on a boat seat early in the morning, are often a good key to the fly to use and the fact that trout will be rising to flies on the surface to make for some great dry-fly fishing.

saltwater fish. Tied in the right size and color, you can fish it for small stream trout or marlin.

My Quick Minnow uses similar translucent tubing. With the right size tubing, you can tie in any size from a 10 to about a 4/0. It also works for any fish that eats minnows or baitfish.

The single most important aspect in picking flies is not to be confused by a fly classification or designation for a particular purpose. For example, trout nymphs are now standard fare when river fishing for small-mouth. Steelhead and Pacific salmon flies work for American shad, and vise-versa. Larger western trout flies take large-mouth, and trout tricos or midges work when carp are taking floating cottonwood seeds. Keep your options open and consider what a fish eats, rather than what name or category is attached to a particular fly.

Imitative Flies Verses Attractor Flies

Anglers tie flies to imitate natural fish food or to imitate nothing in nature—but merely to attract fish. Perhaps a better word than "imitative" would be "suggestive" flies. But just where you draw the dividing line is sometimes difficult.

I think of attractor flies also as "explorer" flies or "exciter" flies—flies that I like to use when blind fishing or casting on new water. They seem best when you are not sure what the fish might be eating, or when you want to elicit a strike to find the fish and then switch to something that is more interesting and closely resembling their food. Attractor flies are often tied in fanciful colors, strange

shapes, with abnormally large or small parts (huge eyes, long wings, too many legs or tails, too long a tail, no tail, lacking legs, etc.), or otherwise not resembling the vaguest suggestion of natural fish food.

Through color, appearance, size, shape, bulk, weight, action or other features, suggestive flies resemble enough of something tasty to make a fish want to eat it. Often, they get better the more they are fished and the more ragged they become. A woolly bugger is a good example. Depending upon the size and colors used to tie it and how you fish it, a woolly bugger can resemble a minnow, leech, hellgrammite, large stonefly nymph, stonecat, sculpin, mad tom, killifish, dace, shrimp, crayfish or numerous other food. You can see in it what you want, but the fish sees in it a meal.

Design Versus Pattern

In years past, the emphasis was on fly patterns. This was when most fly fishing was for trout, perhaps with a little bass thrown in. Early on, trout flies fit the categories such as dry, wet, nymph or streamer. Each fly tie had a specific name, even if the only change was the color of a body or wrap of hackle from an established pattern. The result was a compendium of thousands of flies, which some books have tried to codify.

Perhaps the best of these noble but really fruitless attempts was Don DuBois' 1960 book, *The Fisherman's Handbook of Trout Flies: An encyclopedic guide to wet and dry flies*— including a comprehensive identification list of 5,939 trout fly patterns.

Since then, we have grown more sensible about flies so that we now have designs— rather than patterns—in which a given tying style can be reproduced in many colors, materials, and sizes to create a family of flies.

For fly tiers, this allows for more latitude in tying, and better still, more latitude in thinking. Think bait or fish food when you tie or buy flies, and the results are going to be innovative, imaginative and far better than if held to the orthodoxy of past patterns.

Size

You can throw out a 6-inch-long (15.2-cm) pike fly in a trout stream and I don't care how closely it resembles a native minnow or matches the color of a 2-inch (5-cm) dace, you might as well be fishing in a rain barrel. Throw out a size 12 nymph or little streamer when fishing for big pike and see how many you hook up. Equally ridiculous would be using a large western stonefly nymph on small Eastern trickles for small brook trout, or throwing a big-game fly for breaking, pan-size stripers.

Fly size must match the food size of the expected catch. A friend in Labrador recently landed a lifetime-bragging 7-pound (3.2-kg) brook trout. The trout took a size 2 orange Bomber, which would scare the spots off of any small Eastern brook trout, cozy in a mountain rivulet. Western trout often take size 2, 4 and 6 flies while it's best to fish small stream Eastern trout with size 14s and smaller.

One way to make your own barbless flies for easy release of fish is to use pliers or hemostats to bend down the barb of the fly hook. Use small pliers or hemostats for small flies; large needle-nose pliers for larger flies as shown here.

You must know the size of the food the fish you seek eats to be able to choose the appropriate fly. Small pan-size Chesapeake Bay stripers are going to take size 4 flies and won't even look at the size 4/0 that a Cape Cod striper might engulf. That does not mean that you have to range widely in fly size just because of the wide range of possible fish. For example, with their big mouths and rapacious teeth, a small 1- or 2-pound pike (0.45- to 0.9-kg) might take a size 1/0 streamer, while a 2/0 is plenty large enough for a 35-pound (15.75-kg) trophy pike. As a general rule, big fish eat big prey, since a large meal means less expenditure of energy than chasing down multiple smaller meals.

If you are fishing a lake where the average pike are around 20 inches (50.8 cm), don't use a fly over 5 inches (12.7 cm). If fishing a lake with a number of 30-inch (76.2 cm) pike, try a larger fly (up to 9 inches/22.9 cm). Realize that part of the answer of fly size in this hypothetical situation

Tiny flies (right) are often required for spooky trout, or when trout are taking small nymphs just below the surface or taking tricos or midges on the surface.

Small flies (below) are typical of the imitations for trout stream insects and allow for light tackle and maximum enjoyment when fishing for trout. Flies are available in all different shapes and sizes and to imitate all manner of insects.

Relation of Suckers (Food) and Fish Size

G. H. Lawler, as noted by Mark Sosin and John Clark in their 1973 book, *Through the Fish's Eye,* did research on pike to find the following in the relation of suckers (food) and fish size.

LENGTH, PIKE	LENGTH, SUCKER EATEN	LENGTH, PERCH EATEN
10 inches (25.4 cm)	4 inches (10.2 cm)	4 inches (10.2 cm)
15 inches (38.1 cm)	5 inches (12.7 cm)	4½ inches (11.4 cm)
20 inches (50.8 cm)	5½ inches (14 cm)	5 inches (12.7 cm)
25 inches (63.5 cm)	8½ inches (21 cm)	8 inches (20.3 cm)
30 inches (76.2 cm)	9½ inches (24.1 cm)	NA

involves whether you want quantity or quality catches.

If fishing a lake with 30-inch (76.2-cm) pike, that lake obviously has fish of smaller sizes. Thus, if you fish with a 5-inch (12.7-cm) fly, you have the chance of catching lots of fish 15 inches (38.1 cm) and larger. That means more fish—more quantity—of fish per day. If you fish with 9½-inch (24-cm) flies, most pike will be large, but it also sharply limits your catches of pike less than 30 inches (76.2 cm).

The large fish/large fly concept does not always hold true. Trout take imitative nymphs, dry flies and terrestrials that are very small in relation to their size. American shad to six or more pounds—found on both coasts—take size 6 and 8 flies. Steelhead and Pacific salmon take small bright flies and glo bugs the size of fish roe. Use larger flies for Atlantic salmon. The flies are still small in relation to the size of the salmon.

Shape

In addition to size, shape is the next most important aspect in fish food choice. A striper feeding on sand lance is going to take a skinny, shiny fly that resembles sand lance. That does not mean that you can't fish with a fat dark-banded bulky fly—like a mummichog—and catch a striper when everyone else is taking fish with sand lance flies. But for most fish, most of the time, stick with a fly that resembles what the fish are eating.

Color

A recent article by Woods Hole Oceanic Institution research scientist Dr. David Ross in *Fly Tyer* magazine (Autumn 2005) covers the periodically erupting interest of color in flies. (You can make the same pro/con arguments about color in lures.) Ross has new information on polarized light, fluorescent colors and how they react, along with some information on what different fish see. He also covers the age-old information that different colors change and become darker at different depths.

In his 1984 book, *The Scientific Angler*, Paul Johnson used underwater photos to show how this color loss almost follows the color spectrum, with colors changing to gray and then black (depending upon depth) respectively deep red, red, orange, yellow, green and blue. The exception to this is that colors in shorter wavelengths (indigo and violet) also become darker early, as light penetrates the water.

Once you get deep, the red fly you thought so attractive becomes a medium to dark gray, perhaps even black. The point is that sometimes color matters, sometimes it does not. Some fish, according to research, see color very well, some see less well or mostly in black and white, depending upon the rods (black and white vision) and cones (color vision) in the eyeball.

In his 1961 book, *My Friend the Trout*, Eugene V. Connett included information from an ophthalmologist on the trout eye. Together they found that trout have many rods and cones and could see color very well.

Other research shows that most fish are nearsighted (though sharks are farsighted), that tuna have excellent vision and that inshore coastal fish have good color vision, while offshore pelagic species have poorer ability to differentiate color, but do have good black/white differentiation.

Large flies are suitable for almost any saltwater fly fishing. They range in style and type, but most are in light colors to imitate baitfish and in sizes and shapes that will push water to attract fish.

Fluorescent colors are best on dark days, overcast days, dawn and dusk. This is because there is more of the short UV light at those times, thus bringing out the bright colors of the fluorescent materials. This makes sense when you think about it. Often fluorescent material flies are heavily recommended for steelhead, shad and Pacific salmon. These are fish that hit best early in the morning or late in the evening, or are most active on dark overcast, even rainy days.

At these times, fluorescent materials show up best. It might also closely "match the hatch" with the bright colors and fluorescence similar to the colors found in copepods, mysid shrimp and krill on which these ocean-going fish feed most of the year.

Change color and see if it affects your catch rate. Shad— and perhaps other species under certain situations—will reject a fly that has previously caught a shad in their area. But they will readily strike an identical fly of a different color combination.

Flash

Flash in flies, using such materials as Flashabou, Krystal Flash, Super G Flash, etc, is almost a standard now in a lot of patterns, particularly those for warmwater fish and saltwater species. Flash creates specular highlights that resemble the scales of swimming baitfish, and attracts fish. Flash can even resemble lost scales of fish that have weak scale

Larger, colorful flies are often the best choice for fishingfor big fish ranging from pike to billfish.

attachment, or wounded, scale-shedding fish.

Some streamer fly recipes even suggest tying in flash longer than the hackle wing so that the flash resembles a baitfish losing scales.

Flash has been standard in flies for years, with the addition of metallic tinsel and more recently, Mylar. Thin wire in flash finishes and colors is also becoming more popular for flies. The new flash additions of stranded materials, wire and glitter just add to the possibilities of dressing flies.

Flash can be counterproductive. Shad usually reject a fly that is too flashy. Experiments show that shad do not like a lot of flash, with the possible exception of overcast days or when fishing in early dawn or late dusk.

Relation of Colors with Light Penetration

In their book, *Through the Fish's Eye*, Mark Sosin and John Clark have calculated the retention of colors with light penetration in clear water as follows:

COLOR	10 FEET (9 m)	20 FEET (18 m)
Red	6.5%	0.4%
Orange	50%	25%
Yellow	73%	53%
Green	88%	78%

(Color loss is greater at deeper depths, but most flies tend to be fished shallow rather than deep.)

Large flies are simple, colorful and designed for big-game fishing. Note the popper head on the front of the fly or ahead of the fly to make noise and attract the fish to the fly.

Bulk

Some flies require bulk. This is the philosophy of Dan Blanton, who developed the Whistler series for deep-water fishing. These flies are similar to the Homer Rhode tarpon fly and the Sea-Ducer, but utilize bucktail (not hackle) for the wing and also have bead chain eyes and a chenille body (not seen in Rhode and Sea-Ducer patterns). The thick-wrapped hackle of all three patterns causes them to push water as they are twitched and retrieved.

Fish often can feel or "hear" the fly before they see it. The fish detects the water waves through pores in its lateral line. This is particularly true for the deep-fished Whistler, since the fish has limited vision. Bulky flies help when fishing deep where fish select their next meal not on visual appearance alone, but also on the sound, size and smell of it. Bulky flies can effectively imitate large baitfish.

Weight

Weight added to flies helps the fly angler fish deep—something that is increasingly popular as the boundaries of fly fishing are expanded and as sinking lines are increasingly developed. Weight is often necessary in addition to the sinking lines. Fish a sinking line with a standard wet or submerged unweighted fly on a long leader and the fly will suspend or "float" high in the water column. Use a short leader (to help pull the fly down) with a sinking line to get deep.

You can tie weighted flies in various ways, using lead or non-

Picking a fly is perhaps the most critical choice that you make once you are on the water, since the wrong fly will lead you to believe that there are no fish in the area, when in fact there might be a lot of fish that are just not interested in that fly.

lead (increasingly required with lead-restrictive legislation) products. Possibilities include a wrap of wire, wire tied in parallel to the hook shank, bead chain eyes, dumbbell eyes and metallic cone heads. The best of these have the weight at the head to make the fly dip and yo-yo on retrieve.

A sinking fly has a lot more action this way, action that is similar to a swimming leech and also similar to the up/down movements of baitfish. With tiny amounts of weight added to nymphs for trout fishing, this yo-yo type of action closely resembles the up-down movements of a live nymph and is similar to the up-down movements imparted by dapping a fly and fishing a nymph with the raise-and-drop Jim Leisenring method of wet fly/nymph fishing.

If you are going to fish a lot of weighted flies, consider a system of adding a colored head to the fly to indicate fast sinking or slow sinking. Most flies have black heads, which can indicate no weight. Seal the slow and fast sinking flies with a different color head cement.

Action and Material

The action of a fly and the materials used in that fly go together. In this, we are not talking about the action imparted by a twitch or retrieve of the fly, but the inherent action of the fly itself based on how it is tied and what was used to tie it. The best flies have lots of marabou, rabbit fur, shaggy dubbing and soft hackle that waves with the slightest water movement and causes the fly to look alive.

Sound

Sound is important to fish, since they rely on that as much as vision to find food. And it is a noisy world underwater where sound travels at about five times the speed that it does in air.

You can buy or tie rattle flies. Rattles are available in glass (Venom and others), aluminum (Hart), and plastic (Woodies and others). Of these, I like Woodies plastic rattles since they are easiest to tie to a hook shank without slipping under the thread.

This also relates to the necessity of including a little weight to the front end of a fly to make it sink head first. By sinking this way, it allows the rattle balls to fall to the front of the rattle chamber. When you twitch the fly, you not only cause the fly to swim up, but also cause the rattle to click against the back of the rattle chamber.

For rattles to work, they must be fished this way. It makes no sense to have rattles in a fly that you are going to use for fast strips to breaking fish, in a fly that you drift slowly through a current, or one in which you use an even continuous retrieve. In none of these cases does the rattle make any appreciable noise—and thus adds nothing to the fly or its ability to attract fish.

Strike Factors

Why fish strike can be broken down into several categories:

• Hunger—With any wild animal, including fish, most of their time is spent looking for food. Fish have no system to store food, so they must gather food each day or go hungry. Your fly should represent food.

• Anger—Fish presumably get angry. They might strike out at an invader when defending their space and territory. Fish will get especially defensive when caring for their young or during spawning periods.

• Protection of young—It is well known in bass fishing that a plastic worm cast directly into a spawning bed is usually picked up by the bass and removed from the nest. In this case, the fish are cleaning obstructions or invaders from their nesting area for the protection of their young. Trout get aggressive around their redds. Flies fished in these areas take fish.

Picking out the right fly, as this trout fisherman is doing, can be critical in getting fish to accept the fly and hit.

CHOOSING THE RIGHT FLY

• Instinct—We know that potato chips taste good. When presented with a bowl of them, we might eat even if we are not hungry or had just eaten a full meal. That's instinct, and fish react the same way. It has been said that salmon and shad do not eat once they leave the open ocean and enter a river to spawn. (Some studies indicate that these species occasionally eat in freshwater.) However, it is known that all these species will take flies—perhaps instinctively. They seem to favor flies that imitate their native ocean foods such as krill, mysid shrimp and copepods.

• Curiosity—Fish are naturally curious and move toward something that is foreign to their environment. If their senses tell them that it might act or look like food, then instinct, hunger or habit takes over.

• Competition—Just like a couple of kids all after the same toy in a playroom or hyenas fighting over the best bloody hunk of downed Cape Buffalo—fish compete for food. Most anglers with more than one license have seen fish follow a fly-hooked catch, trying to take the fly away from the hooked fish. That's also a fine time for a second angler to throw a fly into the water to take advantage of this competitive action.

Captured bait (below) such as this (often spit up by a caught fish) is often a good indication of the bait on which fish are feeding and suggestive of the length, shape and color of fly that should be used.

Here (bottom), a baitfish—probably a glass minnow—is in the mouth of a bluefish caught on a fly while feeding in schools of bait.

CHOOSING THE RIGHT FLY

Chapter 4

Casting Tips & Strategies

If you are reading this book, you know the basics of casting. Or perhaps you are reading it to discover tips to correct fly-casting problems. Maybe you want to know how to cast to trout that are farther than 20 feet (6 m) away, bluegills more than 30 feet (9 m) away or bass 60 feet (18.3 m) away. Or you want to know how to get a fly to a sighted tropical fish (bonefish, barracuda, snook, permit—take your pick) without making false casts.

The basics of fly casting are simple, but the details of those basics can be complex. To review Casting 101, think of it not as fly casting, but line casting. The fly, with little weight, just goes along for the ride. The line is the equivalent of the sinker or lure cast when using spinning or bait casting tackle. Since the line is the weight (thus its thickness), you can't just haul off and heave it out there. You can't fling it out without the proper physics in the rod and timing in the cast.

Mending line is critical to getting a good drag-free float of a fly through running water. It must be done as soon as the fly lands, and then repeated as necessary to keep the fly drifting properly.

Proper stance is important, since in any sport—whether tossing a ball, throwing a javelin or making a long cast—you place the foot opposite your casting/throwing arm forward. That way you can lean into the cast (let's stick to fly casting) and punch out a long cast. This obviously becomes more important with long casts and less important with short casts, but it is always important. For right-hand casters, this means that your left foot should be forward of your right.

To cast, you have to move the line. There are two ways to do this. One is by smoothly (but rapidly) jerking the rod upward to cause the line to move like a whip. The second is to not move the rod at all, but to jerk on the line and accelerate it toward you. Do both together the right way, and you will be successful—even if you aren't Lefty Kreh.

Timing of Casts

One of the problems beginners sometimes face is in understanding the timing of casts and the amount of weight the line carries. This does not mean that there is any noticeable weight increase in the line between casts of 20 feet (6 m), 30 feet (9 m) and 40 feet (12 m)—only that there is a change. Current line standards are based on casting an exact 30 feet (9 m) of line (although there is a grain weight plus/minus manufacturing tolerance) so that when casting shorter distances, you are casting less than the weight for which the rod was designed. Casting more line means slightly overloading the rod.

Overloading the rod is not something to worry about. (Using a 4-weight rod with an 8-weight line and picking 50 feet (15.2 m) off the water is

something else again.) In fly-casting, we constantly vary the amount of line out that can be less or more than the 30 feet (9 m) on which lines and rods are balanced.

This varying of the amount of line out also changes the timing of each cast. Basically, we cast by making a backcast, allow the line to drift back and straighten out, and then reverse the casting motion by pushing the rod forward. Proper timing to push the rod forward occurs when the line has straightened. Cast forward too soon and energy of the line can't transfer to the forward cast and the line collapses around you like a knitted doily. Too late, and the line falls on the ground or worse, the line drops, you tick a rock with your fly on the backcast and snap off the hook point.

Timing changes constantly with the length of line. If you are, or are just past beginner

Casting with two anglers in a small boat must be done carefully. One way is to take turns fly casting and to try to keep the line pointed away from the other angler.

Loop control is critical in good casting for both accuracy and distance. In most cases you want a narrow loop in the line, but in some cases (see text) you want a wider loop for specific fishing and fly situations.

stage (or even experienced—there is no law against this) turn around to see what the line is doing to check the best time to push out the forward cast.

Realize that this timing is as rapid as a spinning cast if you have out only a few feet of line past the rod tip, or can be quite a long pause if you are expert enough to carry a lot of line in the air for a distance cast. The important point to know is that timing must change as you cast with more or less line outside of the rod tip.

As your timing and casting distance increases, move the rod farther back to allow more push of the rod for the forward cast. Also, use more of your casting arm and allow the rod to drift back to an angled or horizontal position. This does not mean that you are changing the casting power arc, only that after that power arc, you are drifting the rod back to prepare for the long forward cast.

Loop Control

Throw the rod through a wide arc (angle) and you get a wide loop in the line. Throw a narrow arc and you get a narrow loop. In most cases, you want to cast a narrow loop, for the following reasons:

- The narrower the loop, the more energy that goes into the straight forward direction of the cast and propelling the line forward. The wider the loop, the less rod and line energy that goes to the forward cast and the more energy that goes into making the wide loop.

- The narrower the loop, the less line contact area with the air that it has to push through to turn over.
- The narrower the loop, the more accurate your cast is to hit a specific target.
- The narrower the loop, the less possibility that a gust of wind might blow the line, leader and fly off target.

Once you understand loop control, you're ready to make the arc and the loop in certain prescribed ways. For example, the key to good fishing (fly retrieve, casting control, line control) is to start with the rod tip pointed down at the line or at the water. Then you can control the arc—narrow or wide—without the arc going back and pushing the line and fly down to the ground or water in back of you. A good way to think of your backcast for most fishing is to throw the cast up and back, not just back.

A variation of this for experienced casters is to throw the line back and low, so that you can then throw the forward cast high for maximum distance or a delicate presentation of the falling fly. This low cast must be straight and stay above the water or ground to prevent problems. This is also a rationale for the side-arm or angled-arm cast.

Casting Adjustments

Sometimes specific flies or fishing situations require casting adjustments. An example is with the loop control where a wider loop is beneficial when casting with sinking lines, weighted flies and large flies. It is also helpful when a backcast goes wrong and you need to somehow save the cast and keep the line from landing on you like a cast net. It is also important when you make so narrow a cast with a pushed rod that you tie aerial knots in your line. (The so-called wind knots).

Here are a few situations where you want to adjust your cast, casting arc and loop control:

- Casting instructors constantly preach a "high and back" cast, to keep beginners from dropping the backcast and ruining the forward cast. Part of this is a result of beginners not being able to exert enough accelerated power into the backcast to keep it from dropping. A more advanced technique, where possible, is to keep the backcast strong, forceful and low so that you can throw the forward cast straight and high. This is only possible where you do not have brush in back of you, thus mostly an open water technique. The key is to keep the backcast forceful enough with an accelerated pick up and backcast movement so that the line does not drop and ruin the cast.
- When casting sinking lines, the mass/air resistance ratio of the line is different from that of floating lines. Thus, there is more mass in a smaller space (which is why the line sinks). A typical narrow-loop cast might cause the line loop to become so narrow that it tangles or hits itself to create knots (wind knots).

The solution is to open the arc and the cast just slightly to create a normal or slightly wide loop.

- When casting weighted flies, the fly tends to sink in the air slightly more than a fly that has no appreciable weight. A heavily weighted fly tends to zing back and forth like a thrown stone, making a normal cast dangerous. As a result, a normal cast can cause the fly to drop during the cast and tangle with the line—often on the forward cast. This varies with the weight of the fly, or with the amount of split shot on the leader. Weight in either of these areas causes this problem. To correct this, open the arc to cast a wide loop and to keep the fly higher than normal on a vertical plane cast.
- Some flies tend to sail during a cast. Examples would be some bass bugs and virtually all spoon flies—popular for redfish. Also included are very large and light saltwater flies, often tied with some flattened tubing or flash material. These can tangle with the fly line, and can be dangerous to the caster and friends. To prevent this, use a wider loop to keep the fly higher on an overhead cast.
- To drop a fly gently, like an insect falling naturally on the water, make a high forward cast and aim the cast a few feet above the water. This allows the line, leader and fly to straighten out before settling on the water surface. This creates the effect of an insect blown down to waiting trout.

Casting with split shot requires some special techniques. Here's how to do it: Stop the rod crisply on the backcast, then lower the rod tip slightly to open the loop and give the leader and shot plenty of room to pass the fly line. Allow the line to straighten completely before beginning the forward cast.

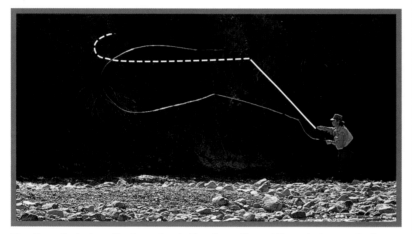

Stop the rod crisply on the forward cast, then lower the rod tip again to open the loop. If you hold your rod in the normal position at the end of the forward cast, the loop will be much tighter (dashed Line), increasing the chance of the line tangling or the weight striking the rod.

- When casting in a meadow, it is possible to catch the fly or line on high grasses during the backcast. To prevent this, do not use a side cast, but use a high backcast and wide-arc forward cast to make a wide high loop that keeps the fly from catching grass or weeds.
- When casting wind resistant flies or bugs, increase the power in your cast. This does not mean that you have to strain yourself, only that you have to use the rod and line (double haul) a little more

than usual. Think of it as using the casting motion/ action/power for a 60-foot (18.3 m) cast when you are actually making a 40-foot (12.2 m) cast. The increased power forces more energy into the cast to turn over a wind resistant fly or bug faster and better. Another alternative is to slightly cut back on the leader (taper or tippet) so that the line energy is transmitted more directly and faster to the leader, tippet and fly.

Shooting Line

Shooting line on the backcast is an advanced technique that makes it possible to load the rod more and also extend the line to get a longer forward cast. You must have the room in back of you for this technique. To do this, make your pick-up off the water more forceful than normal, so that you have excess energy going into the backcast. Aim the line slightly higher than normal so that the line does not fall, touch the water and ruin the cast. Once you do this, allow the power of the backcast to pull the line through your hand to extend the backcast line farther back than normal. Then, with the line back and straight, grab the line to stop the backward flow. Execute the double haul with the rod arc and the pull on the line to load the rod and push the line out in the now-extended forward cast.

You can also shoot line on the forward cast. For this, use a strong forceful forward cast that puts more energy into the cast than that normally used. As the line straightens out in front of you, allow excess line to flow through the guides. Do not allow the line to flow freely, but allow it to flow through a loop made with your line hand thumb and index finger. That way, you can stop the line when you wish to control the cast length. You can also strike a fish if one hits when the fly hits the water.

Form an "O" with the fingers of your line hand after you've stopped the rod. Let the forward cast pull the loose line through your fingers; the "O" will help feed the line through the stripping guide without bunching up or stop the cast if needed. It will also allow striking a fish if one hits as the fly lands.

Dapping

Dapping is not casting, but it is a method of getting a fly to a fish, and doing so very effectively. It can only be done at short distances, since it involves dropping the fly on the water to allow it to drift down through a run or riffle without the line touching the water, or at least not floating on the water surface. You can do this with a dry fly, allowing only the fly (if you are good) or just a little bit of the tippet to float on the water for a drag-free drift. You can also do it with a wet fly or nymph, dropping these weighted flies into the water and controlling the depth and position in the water col-

umn with the rod as the fly drifts with the current.

You can also fish sinking flies with a preset strike indicator, using the floating strike indicator to suggest a take when the indicator slows, stops or dips underwater. This is ideal for small stream trout and obviously best with a long rod (9 feet/ 2.7 m) to control the line and distance of the dapped fly as far from you as possible.

Mending Line

Mending line is the technique of throwing the rod in an arc across a river current to swing cast line from a downstream bellied position to an upstream curve for more of a drag-free float. Do this by getting a snug

line, then flipping the rod in an upstream arc to toss the line up out of the water and in a curve up-current for a long drift and float of the fly.

To do this, mend the line several times during each cast. Start as soon as you make the cast and the line falls across the current. Too many anglers wait until the line starts to belly and the fly starts to race downstream before mending the line. Mending the line at this point never allows you to catch up. The racing fly spooks the fish before you make the first mend. Mending can be done with any floating line in any current situation, but is best with a double taper. Long belly weight forward tapers are the next best choices in line types.

Position yourself as close as possible to the current seam. Place your cast above the rising fish or the suspected lie.

Hold your fly rod out over the seam. This will prevent conflicting currents from pulling your line and creating drag on the fly. The line should come off the rod tip at a right angle to ensure that the weight of the line doesn't pull the fly.

You can't do this with a sinking line, since you are pulling the line off the top of the water, and cannot pull it up from underneath the current.

A variation of mending line is to mend the line downstream.

You never see this written about and it is rare, but it is necessary when fishing a long smooth slow-moving glide with an eddy current between you and the fish in the glide. For this, the fly and leader will float down-

stream, but the counter-current eddy pushes the line upstream. To correct for this and get an even drift of the fly, mend the line downstream to straighten the line as often as necessary for the long glide and fly drift.

CASTING TIPS & STRATEGIES

The Wind Factor

The problem with any wind is that it tends to blow the cast down, but a character of wind is that it is less forceful the closer you get to the ground or water surface. Make a low side cast back into the wind and a high forward cast to use the wind.

From the Back

To make a cast with a back wind, hold the rod low in front of you, and pick up the line, thrusting it sideways into a backcast so that the line loop is parallel to the water surface. As the line straightens out in back and with the rod straight behind you, turn the rod to bring the forward cast up and over your head in a high vertical cast. It helps to use a wide arc to get a wide loop that can be caught by the wind to push the fly the maximum distance. The wind may force you into a shorter than normal side backcast, but you can overcome this with this high forward cast. Naturally, the amount of wind affects the amount of the backcast and your ability to get a good cast from this situation.

From the Front

Wind from the front creates a different, difficult situation. You have two choices. One is to make side casts throughout, trying to keep the line as close as possible to the water or ground surface to lessen the effect of the wind. The second possibility is to throw a high, vertical backcast so that the wind pushes the line back, then make a hard narrow-loop forceful forward cast with a low trajectory.

Make a cast with a narrow arc of the rod for the necessary low trajectory narrow loop control. The forward cast should come in fast, hard and low. Low is particularly important to get the majority of the cast under the wind and less affected by the force of the wind. Normally, you don't want a cast like this, since it tends to slap the fly and line down on the water. In this case, the wind is already riling the water, and you have no choice if you are going to continue fishing.

From the Right

Assuming a right handed caster, a wind from the right is difficult, since it tends to blow the cast on to you, or perhaps a fishing buddy. It can be dangerous, since a wind like this can easily swing a fly hook into you. Wind from the right pushes line to the left throughout the cast. Assuming that you are not near another caster or guide and have some open space, there are two ways to deal with this. One is to make a cross-hand cast by holding your casting hand (right hand) across your left shoulder to make the back and forward casts. Any wind pushes the line away from you, since the rod and line are already to your left. You can't cast as far as normal because of the limited movement of your right arm, but casts of about two-thirds of your normal maximum distance are possible.

The second way to cope with the wind is to turn 180 degrees so that your back is toward your casting target. Make your normal cast, as if you are casting directly opposite your target area. At the final "forward" cast (which becomes the backcast), turn so that you are now facing the target and make the final cast towards the target. Thus, the forward and backcasts are reversed in this final execution. Realize also that on this final cast after the turn, you are now making the cross-hand cast described above, with your right hand across your body. The wind tends to blow the fly off target, so compensation of the target zone is necessary to adjust for the wind blowing the line and fly on the final cast. This cast may blow the line and the fly into other casters who are standing to your left, so use caution or avoid casting altogether if it becomes too dangerous. Left-hand casters must reverse these directions with those following on casting with the wind from the left.

From the Left

The wind from the left blows line away from right-handed casters. Unless you have obstructions or casters to the right of you, this is less of a problem than the cast above. For this, you can cast normally with a vertical overhead cast or angled sidearm cast. Compensate by angling your cast into the wind direction (casting at an angle to the left) on the forward cast so that the wind blows the line to the target zone rather than some distance to the right of it. Avoid this cast if you have companions to your right. Left-handed casters will have to reverse directions with the casting methods for the wind from the right, above.

Backcasting

Proficient fly casting requires putting it all together. That means stance plus a good backcast. Without a good pickup and backcast, a good forward cast is almost impossible. Start with the rod low, and raise the rod in an accelerated arc while pulling on the line to accelerate it also. Continue to accelerate the line as you bring the rod back, propelling the line in back of you in a controlled loop of line until it straightens out. Make sure that you move the rod in a smooth arc to keep the line straight and smooth during the backcast. If the backcast is straight, smooth and level when you complete it, the forward cast will be good. If the backcast is still in a loop, has fallen (both timing errors), curved or slack, then the forward cast will be poor. Look at your backcast and concentrate on it to get a good forward cast.

Double Haul

Knowing the double haul aids in any casting. It allows you to use both hands (rod hand and line hand) for maximum line speed and ease in getting out the line. It reduces your work. It allows faster false casting, which can help getting a fly to a moving fish (such as that mudding bonefish), drying a dry fly before again dropping it in a riffle, keeping your eye on the tar-

Here's how to make a double haul:

Begin the cast (top left) by raising the rod and simultaneously pulling on the line to propel the line to the rear.

Bring your line hand back up immediately (top middle) as the rod accelerates to the rear and as the line rolls out behind you and straightens.

Once the line has straightened behind you (top right), bring the rod forward while at the same time pulling down on the line to add power to the cast for more speed and distance.

As the line rolls out in front of you (bottom right), lower the rod and, if desired, allow additional line to flow through the guides. Use your fingers in an "O" circle to control the line.

Here's how to make a roll cast:

Lift your rod tip slowly until it is slightly behind you and the line is on the water in front of you (top left). Pause momentarily until the line stops moving toward you. This pause lets the water "grip" the line, creating enough friction to load the rod.

Accelerate steadily, make a short speed stroke, then stop the rod quickly (bottom left).

Let the fly line roll out in front of you (below); it should form an elliptical loop and straighten out before falling to the water.

get and hitting it several times in a row for a good fly drift.

Learning the double haul is a little like learning to pat your head and rub your tummy simultaneously. The secret of the double haul is to coordinate your line hand and rod hand so that you use both for maximum acceleration of the line. You can't keep the line from falling (the law of gravity has not yet been repealed) but you can accelerate the line for more speed and distance.

Begin to pull on the line as you pick it off the water with the accelerated arc of your rod hand while raising the rod. This "single haul" as you begin to make a backcast is the same action that in reverse (when making the forward cast)

becomes the double haul. As the line straightens out in back of you, push the rod forward while pulling down on the line to make the double haul. The effect is to accelerate the line through both rod and line movement. There is no real change in the angle or direction of rod movement here—pushing the rod down at this point causes line tangles—"wind knots."

The double haul change in this forward cast is in moving the line rapidly. For this, don't jerk your line arm to the point of rotator cuff problems. Just a little jerk or pull of about a foot (30.5 cm)—done the right way—is enough to accelerate the line with the double haul and give you the needed line speed.

Roll Cast

A roll cast is best done with a double taper line—one of the few situations where a double taper is better than a weight forward taper. If fishing on streams where the bank foliage prevents normal casting and most of your casts are at right angles to the stream flow, get a double taper. To make a roll cast the right way, work out a little line, and then raise the rod to bring the rod in back of you and the line straight toward the target. Most anglers fail on this cast by not bringing the rod back far enough just before making the cast.

By holding the rod just past vertical, you do not get enough of an arc of the rod and transmission of energy into the line to make the cast efficiently. In this case, the line begins to roll out and straighten, but, without the needed energy, lands in a heap at the end. By bringing the rod back farther, you put more force into the cast with the arc of the rod to create the energy for the line to completely straighten out.

Aerial Roll Cast

You can make the same cast as above, but roll the line in the air without it touching the water. The purpose of this cast is two-fold. First, it is the only cast recovery possible with a sinking line, since the line is under the water and you can't pull it off of the water surface as you can a floating line. By making this cast, you can haul the line into a backcast for the next long cast to get the sinking line out. You can also do this with a floating line for the same purpose when you want to pick up the line. To make this aerial roll cast, bring the rod back with only a little in the water, then make a high arcing cast to roll the line out in the air. The difference in execution between this cast and the former standard roll cast is that you are slightly canting the arc of casting force back so that you push the line out high and above the water surface. Timing is critical, since if the line touches the water or straightens out on the water, you then have a "water haul" to pick the line up to make a backcast. The line must be forced into a backcast as soon as the line starts to straighten out in the air.

Side Roll Cast

You can make a side roll cast by executing the cast at 90 degrees to the vertical plane of a standard roll cast. This often works better and makes for an easier cast, particularly for those not familiar with roll casting. For this, hold the rod to the side (parallel to the water) and bring it back behind you so that the curve of the line flowing from the tip top is in back of you. Then switch the rod forward, keeping the rod parallel to the water surface. The result, when done properly, is a cast in which the line rolls out parallel to the water to accomplish

Here are three steps to making an aerial roll cast:

First, raise your rod slowly as the fly passes the lie and while the line is still on the water in front of you. Stop the rod when it is slightlly behind you (left). Accelerate steadily, then make a short speed stroke.

Second, stop the rod quickly while the rod tip is moving in the direction you want the line to go (right). Let the fly line roll out in front of you; it should form an elliptical loop and straighten out above the water.

CASTING TIPS & STRATEGIES

the same result as the standard roll cast.

Distance Roll Cast

You need a distance roll cast when you have no room for a backcast and also need a long cast to get to the fish. For this, pick up the line in a weak cast so that the cast comes back low and close to you. At the end of the energy for this cast, the line is still in front of you and the end of the line touches the water. At this point, you have the same situation as when making a water haul. With the rod in back of you, bring it forward in a roll cast arc to roll the line out. The surface tension holding the end of the line helps load the rod to allow you to make a longer than normal roll cast.

Steeplecast

An alternative to a regular roll cast is the steeple cast. This cast when you have trees or brush behind you, and is a very high backcast that throws the line in back of you and as high as possible to clear any obstructions. This requires fast timing and a quick forward cast to get the line out before it collapses around your ears. It is a sloppy cast, since the line tends to hit hard as you push the rod forward and straighten the line. It is not a good cast for spooky trout; it does work for pond bass, pike and similar fish. It is also good when the water is roiled (waves or raining) or in saltwater when obstructions make it necessary.

Water Haul

One way to help load a rod for a long cast is to use the water haul. This is a part of a cast—not a complete cast—that increases the resistance to picking up the line, thus loading the rod when you have a short line out or need to load the rod when you can't make a long backcast. To do this, allow the end of the line to touch the water and then immediately pick up the line. The line making contact with the surface tension of the water creates resistance to the rod bending, thus loading the rod.

There are several places when you can effectively use this. One is when you don't want to make a roll cast and

Third, make a normal backcast and then a normal forward cast on each cast, and let the line, leader and fly settle to the water.

have some room for a backcast, but not enough room for the length of line you wish to cast. An example would be when wading, but with trees along the bank perhaps 30 to 40 feet (9.1 to 12.2 m) in back of you. You want to make a 60-foot (18.3-m) cast, but don't have the room for a full backcast. For this, make a backcast (it is best to watch this step by turning to see the line) and allow the line end to just barely touch the water. At this point, bring the rod forward in a high forward cast motion. The surface tension of the water holds, then releases the line after the rod is loaded to allow making the desired long cast. You can also use this to make a backcast when you have out only a short line, by picking the line off of the water with the end still held by the water surface to load the rod for the backcast. This tends to rip the line off the water—bad when there are fish in the area that easily spook. A third way to use this technique is with a distance roll cast, as described above.

Change-of-Direction Cast

Another advanced cast for the trees-in-back-of-you situation is the change-of-direction cast, which purports to allow you to change the direction of a cast to a 90-degree angle from the shoreline. You can't do this, but you can get the cast to about a 60- to 70-degree angle with the bank. To make this cast, make forceful false casts along the shore (parallel to the bank) and then on the last forward cast, turn the rod sharply

at 90 degrees to point straight out towards the water. The result is that the line follows the tip of the rod to make an almost, but not quite, 90-degree change of direction to get the fly towards the target area.

Lazy-S Cast

One of the problems of fishing current in rivers and streams is that current in the middle is faster than where you are wading and faster than where you want to fish. It is not uncommon to have to reach across a fast current to attempt a drag-free float to a fly, dry or wet. One way to do this is with a lazy-S cast, which describes the zigzag line that results.

The purpose is to cast a series of back-and-forth curves that flow with the current, while not affecting the fly, which can go through a lengthy drag-free float. This cast, and the resultant drag-free float, is only as good as the size of the curves cast, the speed of the current and width of the current that you have to cross with the line. Eventually, drag takes over and pulls the fly downstream.

To do this, cast normally, but on the final forward cast, rapidly shake the rod side-to-side to create waves in the line. Little shakes make little waves of line; rapid or bigger shakes of the rod make bigger waves of line. You can also make these at the beginning of the forward cast to create waves at the end of the line. By making shakes throughout the final cast, you create waves all along the cast line. Shakes at the end of the cast create curves in the line closest

to you. When a fish hits, you have more slack line out as a result of this and must react accordingly. This is not a useful cast in tidal saltwater situations (there is little variation in tidal current) unless you are fishing close to a bank where the tidal flow slows.

Pile Cast

Also known as a dump cast, a pile cast is another way to get a slack end of the leader close to the fly to get a drag-free float. Anglers often use it with dry flies, but you can also use it for drag-free floats of wet flies and nymphs. It won't take the place of the lazy-S cast, which you will still use on larger water, but it's an ideal cast for small streams and pocket water situations. In essence, what you want is a little bit of slack in the line leader next to the fly so that the slack line can wash out while the fly drifts free. There are two ways to do this. One is to add an additional tippet length to the end of the leader so that the fly cannot completely turn over, allowing the fly to land with a "pile" of leader tippet near it to wash out while the fly drifts. A second way is to cast forcefully, and then stop the forward movement of the line to cause the leader end to spring back and pile up. In making this cast, aim and cast farther than the target, since the leader springs back to hit the target short.

Tuck Cast

Use a tuck cast to sink a weighted nymph or wet fly. To do this, make a forceful forward cast. At the end of the cast, slightly pull back and raise the rod or drop your rod hand to cause the force of the cast to propel the fly down, hitting the water before the leader or line, and immediately sinking.

Side Loop Cast

Often fly fishing requires an upstream cast to a fish, and a curve in the line or leader to present the fly in front of a rock or around some obstruction. This cast also allows presenting a fly to a fish in open water without lining the fish and scaring it into the next county. There are several ways to make casts so that the leader ends up angled to the right or left of the cast direction.

One way to make a side cast is to figure the distance to the target area and then work out a little more line to allow for the side angled cast. Make the cast and at the end of the cast, turn the rod tip towards the direction that you want the leader curve. The leader follows the rod tip action. This also makes it easy to make the cast to the right or left—simply by adjusting the rod tip movement. You can also make a side cast, using more or less force in the cast to cause the line to curve. If right-handed, turn the rod to make a side-armed cast and then make the cast, but make it more forceful than needed for the length of the line/leader out. The result is that the leader end whips around from the excessive force and creates a left hand curve. (This is the same principle used with the tuck cast.) Make the same cast, but with a weak forward cast, while still carrying the line above the water, and the line/leader will fall before the cast completely straightens, creating a right-hand curve. Left-handed casters can reverse these actions for similar casts around an obstruction.

Practice, Practice, Practice

The best way to become an advanced caster is to practice. Pros in other sports practice constantly. The best practice of various casts is on water. If water is not available, practice on the lawn, but use an old line. The only casts that you can't do on the lawn are the water haul and the various roll casts, since there is no water surface tension to hold the line for making the cast. You can improve other casts through regular practice in your back yard.

Choose a practice surface of water or grass with no trees nearby to interfere with your line (above). Avoid casting over surfaces such as gravel or asphalt, which can damage your line.

Tie a piece of fluorescent yarn to the end of your leader in place of a fly (near right). The yarn won't snag, is safer than a sharp hook and helps you see the end of your leader in the air and on the ground.

Practice accuracy, which is often more important than distance. Use a paper plate or plastic hoop as a casting target (far right). Position targets at various distances and practice placing the end of your leader onto each target.

Chapter 5

Reading Freshwater—
Streams, Rivers, Ponds, Lakes

Rocks and riffles are ideal spots to fish in a stream, but it is important to understand the nature of the quiet or buffer areas of holding waters around these rocks and obstructions.

Understanding water and the differences among types of water are among the keys to finding fish. Finding fish is the key to catching fish.

The key to any fishing is to fish where the fish live. This has to be considered in a horizontal plane. Where in the expanse of any stream/river/pond/lake are fish likely to live? It also involves the vertical plane. Where in the water column—top to bottom—will the fish be located? This is affected by the type of water, also the species of fish (free-ranging like trout in a pond or structure-oriented like bass) along with the season of the year and even the time of day.

Beginners often start fishing without a clear idea of where fish are located. It pays to examine the water (read the water), learn the habits of the fish sought, understand fish movements for the season and then fish accordingly.

You can take any body of water—pond, lake, section of big river or small stream—and lay out imaginary grid lines. Some of the resulting imaginary grids are going to hold fish all of the time, some hold fish part of the time, and some never hold fish unless a fish is moving from point A to point B through that grid. The same applies to the vertical water column, where fish will move up and down depending upon their basic needs.

Fish need the basics to live— oxygenated water, cover, access to food, comfort, the right temperature, and protection from enemies. Fish are just like people, only wetter. In addition, different species vary in their needs for cold water, oxygen, food, spawning sites and other needs. Salmon and trout need colder water than other species,

carp feed mostly on the bottom, smallmouth like crayfish, trout eat aquatic nymphs, largemouth bass like wood structure holding areas, trout need higher levels of oxygen than carp, crappie like to school in brush piles, pike eat large suckers, bluegills eat aquatic bugs, pike favor still water and weeds, and the list goes on and on. Knowing these seemingly disparate facts about fish and fish areas can make the difference in the size and numbers of fish caught.

Basics of Reading Water

The key to reading running water is to look for spots that offer protection, comfort, shade, access to food and cover from predators. No fish likes to swim against a current all the time, just as we would not want to walk or jog constantly. The hydraulics of water is such that

any structure in moving water (bottom, sides, banks, rocks, riffles, boulders, logs) creates a buffer area of protected or quiet (or slower moving) water that is more comfortable for fish. Fish still get all the oxygen that the specific water flow holds, they still have access to food that is drifting by, but they do not have to fight the current 24/7.

This buffer area varies with the size and type of the structure and the type of current. A simple round rock, protruding from the surface, has a buffer area in front of, on both sides of and in back of the rock. As a result of the water force, the largest buffer area (or "tail" of protected water) is on the down-current side of the rock. That tail area of protected or buffered water is larger and longer on a large boulder than on a small rock. If the rock is underwater, then there is also a buffer area on the top of the rock. Rocks of varying sizes and

Reading freshwater streams includes taking advantage of various structure types, such as casting around a bridge piling that will likely be a holding spot for fish.

shapes will have different configurations of buffer areas.

This does not mean that you find fish randomly spaced around all of these areas. The buffer area in front of a rock is relatively thin and fish need to face into the current. That means that a fish might have its tail in the buffer area, but would have to have most of its body in the fast current, defeating the purpose of that position. It is better for the fish on the side of the rock, since they can hug against the rock and remain in the protected buffer water while still on the alert for drifting food. It is particularly good where the rock meets the stream bed, since this is the conjunction of two buffer areas. It is also especially good in back (down current) of the rock, since this

is the largest protected area and one that provides the most comfort, easy maintenance in the fast moving stream and access to food. Look at any rock like this in fast water and you also see a seam or edge where the fast water rushing by the rock meets the down current buffer area.

Just because a protected buffer area exists on top of an underwater rock does not mean that you will find fish there. This is an area—particularly in a shallow stream with no overhead tree cover—that is very vulnerable to predation by hawks, ospreys, owls, coyote, fox or bear. It is also an area in full sun, something that most fish try to avoid both for eye comfort (they don't have eyelids they can shut) and for body temperature.

There is also good "structure" all along the bottom. The bottom provides the same buffer protection because the quietest water in any stream is anywhere the water runs adjacent to some structure (in this case, the bottom of the stream), while the fastest current is in mid-current, slightly under the surface.

The holding ability of any type of bottom varies for fish and the number of fish located there. A plain, relatively even gravel bottom is not as good for holding fish as is a pool bottom with pockets, larger rocks, shelf rock, ridges, logs and tree stumps. Reading "through" the water to try to decipher the bottom structure in those shallow streams goes a long way to finding where fish live—and where to catch them.

Tailwater streams, fed by cold water from the depths of a reservoir, often hold large trout populations, including many fish of trophy size. The best tailwater streams have stable flows, allowing development of rooted vegetation that holds many aquatic insects. Trout are not as numerous in tailwater streams where the water level fluctuates greatly as water is released to drive power generator turbines. These fluctuations limit insect populations and trout reproduction.

READING FRESHWATER

Meandering streams (left) have diverse trout habitat; channelized streams (right) have uniform habitat.

Types of Water

Where fish live depends upon the type of water. While it is an oversimplification, you can divide freshwater fly fishing possibilities into four categories—streams (such as those for trout, spawning steelhead, ends of shad runs), rivers (smallmouth, largemouth, catfish, steelhead, Atlantic salmon, Pacific salmon, shad, stripers), ponds (largemouth bass, catfish, carp, panfish, crappie), and larger lakes or reservoirs (largemouth bass, smallmouth bass, panfish, crappie, catfish, walleye, carp, catfish, pike, drum, pickerel, muskie).

Think of your own home waters, and place them into one of these basic categories. Realize that every description—

as follows—has a built-in local bias. For many from the northeast, a stream is no wider than a two-lane road. To those from the west, a pond might be a few hundred acres or more, which is a lake to most mid-Atlantic anglers. An angler might describe a river as huge or small, deep or shallow, fast flowing or slowly meandering.

Waters can also have different character depending upon the geography and elevation. A river in the east might be wide, shallow and with a reasonable gradient of flow—typically, a smallmouth river. In the south, that river might be slow and meandering, below the fall line or in a flood plain. These southern rivers are ideal for catfish, largemouth and bowfin. In the west, you will find rivers big, rough, deeper and wilder. When

you arrive in season, you'll find the western rivers full of shad, steelhead or several species of Pacific salmon.

Lakes and ponds can have similar differences along with many similarities. Ponds in the east are typically farm ponds—pastoral and calm—home for bluegills, other sunfish and largemouth bass. In the Midwest, add some catfish. In the north (Michigan and Wisconsin) or at high elevations (Colorado) you won't find farm ponds, but keep an eye out for a beaver dam, some larch, aspen or other high country trees. Find some downed logs, a couple of rocks and a weed bed or two and you have a home for cutthroat trout, maybe some grayling and rainbows or even golden trout.

The amount of running water can also affect fishing.

Streams

You might think of streams as waters that you can mostly wade with hip boots. Or you might think of them as tributaries of larger rivers. I think of these streams as filled with rocks, boulders, pockets of weed beds, small bridges, plunge pools, riffles, long pools and runs, undercut banks and downed timber. Some of these trout streams are in high-mountain or hill country with a fast drop and a lot of plunge pools and waterfalls.

Other streams might be in meadows or lowlands, such as the limestone streams in south central Pennsylvania made famous by the likes of Charlie Fox, Vince Marinaro and others. These are streams that are typically trout water, although in some warmer areas, they might more typically harbor sunfish or a few smallmouth and catfish. Small streams like this that hold warmwater species also exist throughout the country and are extensively found in the Midwest.

All the basics of running water hydraulics apply to streams. These same basics also apply to fish holding in other areas of fast water streams such as an undercut bank, alongside a boulder, next to a downed log, adjacent to a bridge piling or other such place. The bottom is good also. It is often on trout stream bottoms like this that you can spot flashes as trout twist and turn to get nymphs, exposing their light-colored bellies.

Eddies or back-currents are also good, since they provide food, shelter and a quiet area. The difference with eddies is that they are counter-currents to the main stream flow, so that fish are facing into the current of the eddy, not facing upstream as the stream current is flowing. Depending upon the size of the eddy and the position of the fish, you could have fish facing upstream, downstream, side-ways to the stream flow, but always into the eddy current.

No stream is a straight tube or channel (except for those that the Army Corps of Engineers or other government agency has made into a channel). This means that all streams (and also rivers or other flowing freshwater) have twists and turns of current, fast and slow flows, shallow gravel bars, narrowing gorges, wide pools, turns with deep holes on one bank, upwellings from the bottom, springs, waterfalls, plunge pools, swirls and whirlpools. These currents can change as the water volume changes during periods of drought or high water from rain and snow runoff.

Some structure of streams is good even when there is relatively little direct downward current. An example is a plunge pool (minor waterfall) or a major waterfall where the force of the water is straight or angled down into the stream or

Pools like this, with a small tributary coming into it to provide cool oxygenated water, are ideal for fly fishing. Often the best fishing is right around the tributary mouth as this fly angler has found in his search for trout.

pool—not horizontal with the main current of the stream. This brings a lot of oxygen into the pool along with mixing the water, in time digging out a deep hole that is attractive to larger fish. These are ideal places to fish.

It is best to approach streams like this one pool at a time. Fish each pool thoroughly before moving on to the next pool. It is also best to move upstream so that you are always behind the trout to prevent them from seeing you as you cast. Depending upon the pool and the stream, this might be a small plunge pool the size of your living room rug or a large pool the size of a long home driveway. In all cases, examine the pool first to check out the possibilities for fish holding spots. This might be any of the above listed areas. Then work from the tail of the pool towards the head of the pool to avoid fish spotting you.

Rivers

Think of rivers as large streams, since they have the same characteristics as streams, just more water. The same hydraulics of all moving water and streams apply to rivers, just on a grander scale. The larger size and heavier water flow generally mean deeper water, longer pools, more rocks and riffles so that you may need to travel in a boat or canoe, as well as wading in shallows or along the shore.

Rivers can vary from those deep waterways that drop off immediately and do not allow any shore or wade fishing, to those that are very shallow and allow wading throughout much of their length and width. They can have a fast water flow, such

as northwest waters typical for trout, salmon, shad and steelhead; or a slow meandering flow such as those in the south and Midwest, where you are likely to find bass, drum, walleye and catfish.

You can often find such varying waters in nearby geographic areas. For example in my area of the mid-Atlantic, we have the lower section of the "mile wide and a foot deep" Susquehanna, which lends itself to jon boat fly fishing and shallow wading for smallmouth bass. Less than 150

miles away on the lower eastern shore, we also have the Pocomoke, rated as one of the deepest rivers in the world for its width and good for largemouth bass and gar.

Some anglers find big rivers intimidating, particularly those who have only fished still-water ponds or small streams. The secret of dealing with the larger water is to break it down into small parts. Think of the river in terms of sections and fish each section thoroughly. By working such a spot thoroughly and

In some fishing such as this fishing and catch of a west coast American shad, the best areas for fishing are around the tails of pools to catch these migrating fish as they come up the river or stream.

gaining confidence and some catches, you have the ability to attack other sections of the river and concentrate on the areas that hold fish.

In deep-water rivers, you still have the bottom structure and deep rocks of small rivers and streams—you just might not see them. Most likely, you will find it more difficult to fish them, since fly fishing requires deep sinking lines to get a fly into the strike zone. But you don't have to blind fish in open water. There are weed beds and blow downs along the shore, cypress knees, trees, stumps, log jams, beaver dams, rocks and man-made structures like docks and piers. Since most fish like structure, particularly largemouth, pike, sunfish and gar, these man-made structures are the equivalent of the rocks and natural structure of other rivers. These are the best spots to fish.

Ponds

I like to think of ponds as miniatures of lakes and reservoirs. Ponds vary in that some exclusively harbor coldwater species, others only warmwater species. Usually, you find beaver ponds and such in the North Country filled with basic trout and grayling, while the farm ponds of the Midwest and small sloughs of the south are typically home to bass and sunfish.

Ponds are shallow, varying from a fraction of an acre (rare) to several or more acres in size. These are nothing more than a collection of structure types that vary with each part of the country. Man-made ponds are bowl-like since they are made using a bulldozer in a small stream bed to carve out a pond. Workers then use that dirt to make an earthen dam on the down current side of the stream that will fill the pond. In time,

the ponds fill with weeds along the shore, and might have a boat dock or two, overhanging brush or trees, standing timber, downed logs, brush piles, gravel bars or patches of pads. One shore may even have a bluff or rock ledge.

Since most of these are man-made and stocked with warmwater species (like catfish, largemouth bass and bluegill or other sunfish), think of the wood structure and weed beds as the hot spots for fish. Many ponds are nothing more than collections of structure. Even though there is no running water as in a river or stream, most fish still like the comfort of structure for their living quarters.

You can fish many small ponds from shore. Fishing from shore is often best. This is true if the pond is small (a few acres or less), or if a boat or canoe is not available.

Streams and rivers with extreme gradients are often difficult to climb around, but create deep plunge pools that can hold big trout.

Lakes

Lakes can be intimidating. They can range in size from a few hundred acres, to many thousands of acres. Lakes can be deep and cold like the Great Lakes; they can have bays and weedy coves like the pike lakes of Canada. Spanish moss hanging from live oak trees border lakes in the south. Tundra and lichens border lakes in the north, where pike and muskie are the typical quarry.

Where do you start? You don't start in the middle—unless that middle is shallow with a submerged weed bed, has an underwater rocky hummock or sports a grass-bordered island.

The main difference between lakes and ponds is that in a lake everything is bigger. Where you might have a cove the size of a rug on a small pond, a cove on a lake might be the size of a football field. Other than that, they could be similar. Both can be the same shallow depth, with the same weeds, log jam, rock shelf and with the same species of fish. There is just a whole lot more on a lake.

That can be both good and bad. With more structure and places to fish, and larger areas, you have more possibilities to take fish, and can have more productive fishing time. But on a small pond with one stump, you know that the best bass in the pond is going to be near that stump. In a lake with a hundred stumps in a huge cove, you can have more fish, but you probably don't know which stump is the best, which stumps do or don't hold fish and which stump holds the biggest and smallest bass. You just have to fish the stumps a lot and work the water methodically to check the structured areas.

If it seems I am stressing shallows a lot, there is a reason. Most fly fishing, even with the sinking lines—that sink no faster than about 10 inches (25.4 cm) per second (a far cry from a free-falling jig)—we are fishing shallow. Vertical jigging, a common term with anglers for getting a structure spoon or lead head jig deep, does not apply and has no equivalent in fly fishing.

There are also other differences between lakes and ponds. Generally lakes have a lot of structure and components not found in ponds, unless the ponds are very large. Some lakes have islands, which increases the shallows and the shoreline area of the lake. Often these islands have the same features as the rest of the lake, including points, grass beds, log jams, standing timber, stumps and rock bluffs.

An underwater island, which shows on a depth finder, is another possible place to find fish. If it is shallow enough so that sunlight can reach the bottom, it will have grass beds that hold fish. While warmwater lakes and coldwater lakes are different, both trout and bass are possibilities for these spots. These underwater islands might also be rocky or have standing timber or stumps, particularly if the lake is a flooded man-made reservoir. These structures hold fish.

Typical lakes stratify during the summer, with a turnover in the fall. This summer stratification forms three layers to the lake—the top epilimnion, the center thermocline and the bottom hypolimnion. This is actually good for fly anglers, since the bottom hypolimnion in this stratification has little oxygen, cold temperatures and holds few fish and less life than other parts of the lake. The top epilimnion layer gets hotter as the summer progresses and also has a decrease in oxygen except when storms and wind stir the surface and mix the water. The middle level—the thermocline—has rapidly dropping temperatures which fish find cooling during hot summer months. It also has a fair amount of oxygen to sustain aquatic life. Fishing from the top down to this thermocline level provides the best fishing, regardless of the tackle. It is also best for fly fishing, since even with sinking lines the fishing is easiest and best in the top layers of water.

Concentrate on one section or shoreline area and fish that thoroughly when you read a lake—don't let the whole expanse of the water intimidate you. For example, you might have a shoreline of weeds and emergent grasses that you can fish for pike or trout, depending upon the lake. You might have a cove filled with stumps or standing timber, which has the potential of holding a bass or two by each piece of structure.

You might find a point of land extending into the lake. During the early bass spawning period, this could hold bass beginning to make beds. Other possibilities to find fish are bridge pilings, docks, boat houses and piers, standing timber found on flooded lakes, log jams from timbering, extensive weed beds, rock piles, rock cliffs, steep drop-offs, underwater caves, rocky outcroppings, channels, old road beds and so on.

Chapter 6

Reading Saltwater— Bays, Estuaries, Coves, Tidal Rivers, Coastal, Inshore

Often tropical flats will hold fish that are easy to spot as they tail or fin working the flat for food. Here, John Randolph of *Fly Fisherman* magazine crouches as he makes a presentation to a bonefish (foreground).

First glance at a saltwater fishing spot can be even more intimidating than a look at a large lake. The whole ocean— or bay or tidal river— is out there. Where do you start? The answer is that you start with known structure or known areas of fish activity, looking for signals that indicate where to throw a fly. There are differences between saltwater and freshwater, with tidal flows constantly changing the fishing picture.

Tide

The moon (along with a few dozen other factors) controls tides. Tides create a change in water level and currents approximately two times each day (two complete tidal changes occur approximately every 25 hours). Basic tides change about every 6 1/2 hours, with a dead low and dead high at each tidal change.

Tides bring new bait into areas, disturb bait for the advantage of gamefish, flush out waste and waters, help drain or slow the draining of tidal rivers, change the levels of water and alter fishing conditions. Tides flood mud banks during a high tide, creating shallow-water fishing. Anglers can reach deep holes with a fly during low tides.

Tides are created when the moon and body of water on the earth are closest and again farthest away (on the opposite side of the earth). One basic rule for saltwater fishing in tidal areas is that there is little fishing success during dead high and dead low periods as the tide shifts. There are also higher and lower than normal tides, called spring tides (they "spring" forth, thus the name) and neap tides. Spring (very high) tides occur on the full and new moons, while neap (very low tides) happen on the first- and third-quarter phases of the moon.

Running tides move bait and bait attracts fish. Running tides also cause changes in the sea level along coastal areas. A low tide might expose a flounder slough or skinny bonefish flat that is good on a high tide. Conversely, a surf slough for stripers or a wading flat for redfish that is great on a low tide might be too deep to fish during high tide. A high tide might hold snook back in the mangroves, while a low tide might push them to the edge of the mangroves or to a new area.

Tidal flows are best in shoreline areas where the tide runs past protected spots like jetties, sandy points, bridge pilings, docks, and channel markers that create "seams." These seams—edges of calm water and fast tidal flows—allow fish to hold in a protected area, but swing out and grab food the tide pushes by. Here, tides are just like river currents, except that they change direction twice a day.

With these tidal flows, saltwater species generally seek protected waters where they can rest while still grabbing food pushed by the tide. Protected areas around docks, piers, bridge pilings, channel markers and such are no different from a rock in a trout stream or a log in a largemouth river. All allow fish to rest and still take food pushed along by the current. The main difference here is that the tide changes twice a day so that for any structure, you get two tidal flows going in one direction and two in the other during any 24-hour period. This means that a fish that is holding on the east (buffer) side of structure during an east-flowing tide will shift positions and be on the west side as the tide flows west some 6 1/2 hours later.

Tides will also affect the salinity of a tidal river area, and this can affect the numbers of species of fish that you get in an area. If you have a slow tidal river and an outgoing tide, there is less likelihood of true saltwater species holding in that area. As the tide comes back into the river bringing with it saline waters, the saltwater species will follow.

Bonefish like this one caught in Mexico by Brenda Pfeiffer and guide Alberto are easily spotted on tropical flats, but require a stealthy approach and careful cast to get the fly to the fish.

Natural Structure

Natural structure is any structure that is natural to the area and that helps hold fish. It can be anything from weeds to coral reefs, channel edges to skinny flats.

Coves

Coves are naturally sheltered areas, often with a lot of bait. These are places that usually have grassy shorelines and shallows. They serve as protected areas for smaller species (read food, if you are a fish) and serve as a nursery for gamefish. Crabs, grass shrimp, mummichogs, glass minnows, bay anchovies, baby eels, and other food fish inhabit areas like this. Coves are a natural cafeteria for gamefish and a perfect area to fish. They are also more protected from the wind than open water situations and make for easier fly-casting.

Coves can be large or small, with the smaller ones often the best in that they tend to hold more fish, have less disruptive boat traffic and are easier to figure out and fish. When fishing any cove, look for both natural and man-made structure.

Tidal Rivers

Tides affect tidal rivers, which are found in coastal lowlands. These rivers usually have brackish water and often have a mix of fresh and saltwater species of gamefish. These are also large gathering areas for fish, and contain both natural and man-made structures that hold fish. Prime among these are bridge pilings, docks, channel markers and the like that serve as buffer areas. Depending upon the time of the month, the force of the tide and the distance in the river from the main salt tidal forces, this tide may be strong or weak, but often with only slight differences in height between the high and low. In tidal rivers, the natural current of the river is aided by an outgoing tide, while it will fight an incoming high tide flow.

Reefs

On the north coasts of the Atlantic and Pacific, you find reefs. In some areas you find remnants of the oyster beds and bars of the past. Both are reefs and both hold fish. Any protected natural structure like these has the same attributes of any structure—algae and grass growth that are home to minnows or mussels, and a protected area and cafeteria for gamefish. They also provide protected buffer water for gamefish, making these ideal spots to fly fish thoroughly. While oyster reefs originally touched the high tide mark, today most are gone as a result of commercial oystering. Sinking lines are a must to fish these deep rock reefs and oyster beds effectively.

Rocky Shorelines

This example of natural structure is found more in northern coastal areas than in the south. They also provide a natural area for food and shelter. Rocks along the shore break up tidal flows and the resultant waves help mix oxygen in the water. They also provide the basis for the food chain by providing anchors for grasses and weeds, shelter for baitfish, minnows and mussels, and protection for gamefish. The main thing that rocky shorelines provide is a cafeteria of food choices. As a result, these are ideal places to fly fish. Only rarely can you fish them from the shore, since the wave action makes controlling the fly and line difficult if not impossible, and attempts to land any caught fish difficult or dangerous. Boat fishing systematically along a rocky shore does allow careful casts to the base of the rocks to cover all possible gamefish spots.

Sandy Sloughs

Sloughs are nothing more than a slight or deep depression in an otherwise flat inshore bottom. As a result, they can be good on either a high or low tide, depending upon the slough. When boat fishing, you can detect sloughs on a depth finder and use fishing markers to outline the fishing area. You can also scout an area during low tide to find "pockets" in bare or very shallow flats to find high tide sloughs. Flounder and other bottom species move out of these areas during a low tide, but move right back in on a high tide.

Surf Sloughs

These are depressed areas between the beach and a bar several to several hundred feet (meters) out. They are ideal for the surf fly angler to reach and usually easy to reach from the shore. You'll find surf sloughs right off of the beach that can host everything from feeding puppy drum to breaking bluefish to false albacore zipping through the suds to take minnows. The best fishing is when you have fish actively feeding in sloughs, often indicated by diving birds.

Surf Bars

Bars are high points in an otherwise flat bottom. They seldom have fish on them, but are good keys for finding fish in the deeper water to the sides or in adjoining sloughs.

Surf Cuts

These are depressions in the bottom between two bars that make "gateways" for fish moving from outside of a bar to close inshore to feed on sand crabs, baitfish and minnows. To find these, look for gaps in the waves breaking, or a difference in the way the waves are crashing on the shore. Gaps in the pattern of breaking waves indicate cuts—ideal places to throw a sinking fly on a sinking line to attract stripers, bluefish, sea trout and sometimes even little tunny that move in and out of these areas. Realize that these—along with sloughs and cuts—may change throughout a season and particularly after any bad storm.

Inlets or River Mouths

The junction of tidal rivers and the bay or ocean is an ideal place to find fish. The river brings bait downstream to the waiting fish, while the change in tides mixes the water, disorients bait and makes for easy picking by any gamefish. Inlets can be large or small, safe for all fishing or decidedly dangerous with the mix of an incoming tide and outgoing river flow. In addition, large inlets can be channels from upriver ports and marked with buoys and channel markers for boats. If fishing in these areas, prepare to give way to sailboats, unless you are anchored (but remember that you cannot anchor in a channel). It is illegal to tie up to any channel marker or buoy. The mix of water sometimes makes it hard to determine a specific current so a drift of a fly is often difficult. These are still good areas to fish and often birds in these areas indicate breaking fish.

Rip Lines

These are seams between two currents or types of water. Often these result from changes in tides or a tide and a river mouth current, where you can have waters of two different salinities, temperatures or even current speeds. Foam or small amounts of flotsam on the surface can indicate rip lines. These are ideal to fish, working both sides of the rip to take gamefish that are feeding on bait.

Coral

Coral reefs are fragile environments and yet hold a lot of fish. They are reefs of animals that have built up over time and in turn attract sea weed, plants, small baitfish, and gamefish feeding on the bait. Because they are fragile, do not get out and walk on them–even if they are showing on the surface. Similarly, do not anchor, since this will damage them. The best way to fly fish them is to use a fly line sufficient to reach the top of the reef and drift through the area, using a GPS unit to determine where you are for a return trip. Another way to fish is to use a fast sinking line and fish the edge of the reef, either working parallel to the edge of the reef or drifting so that you can make repeated casts to allow a fly to sink along the coral reef face.

Channels

Red and green Coast Guard markers mark channels that you can fish, but it is illegal to anchor in these areas. Often the best place to fish is along the edge of these channels where shallows meet the deeper water.

Flats

We typically think of flats as tropical places to find bonefish, permit, sharks and barracuda, but you can have flats that will hold feeding fish in any area during certain tides. Flats can be good or bad depending upon the tide. Local knowledge of

Author with a nice redfish hooked as soon as the fly landed—ample reason to keep the line in your line hand at all times.

when flats are good is paramount to be able to fish them effectively. In most cases flats must have at least a foot (30.5 cm) of water to hold fish, even though in that shallow water, fish fins and tails might stick out as they grub along the bottom. Those fins and tails are one way to find actively feeding fish.

Blue Holes

This term is sometimes used for the deep holes, large openings, and basins that are found in large coral reefs. As such, they often provide an opportunity to take large fish—like tarpon, barracuda, grouper and amberjack—that would be difficult to take elsewhere on a reef or not in the large sizes of fish found in these areas. The difficulty is that they are deep openings that, in turn, are surrounded by coral. Most fish hooked in these are lost, often with the line and backing. If they are large, they may be worth a try to take a trophy, casting sinking lines and large flies. If they are not large enough for the fish to run, or with an opening that will allow the fish to get to the open sea, they may be worth it for the brief thrill of a big fish hooked, but might be costly in terms of line and backing.

Weed Beds

These vary from the eel grass and celery grass of shallow East coast areas to

Choosing the right fly can also include the presence or absence of a weed guard, such as on these snook flies. These are necessary for fishing close to the mangroves where snook hide in tropical regions.

the huge kelp beds off Catalina in California. They all hold bait and gamefish. Often the key to fishing areas like this is to fish the outside edges where you will not snag weeds with the fly, or fish in areas with sparse weed growth so that you can weave a fly through the weeds. Fishing thick weeds where you get hung up as soon as you start a retrieve won't get you any strikes, even if the fish are stacked up.

Mangroves

Tropical mangroves are havens for snook, tarpon, barracuda, mutton snapper, mangrove snapper, sharks, sea trout, ladyfish and similar tropical species. The mangroves themselves are good for snook, the cuts between them are good for tarpon and the outside edges are good for snapper. Tides also affect mangroves. A high tide might flood a mangrove flat and push the fish back into the roots where they are impossible to reach. A low tide on the same flat can push snook out and keep them along the edge, or move them to a different stand of mangroves that has deeper water on a low tide.

Man-Made Structure

Man-made structure is any structure created by people, including bridges, pilings, docks, oil rigs or buoys.

Bridge Pilings

Bridge pilings can be thick or thin, scattered or clustered, but they are always good spots to fly fish. Any man-made structure placed in the water in a short time collects algae, moss, grasses, clams and mussels, and serves as a gathering point for small fish and minnows. This attracts gamefish and also provides gamefish protection from the tidal currents. The buffer water around bridge pilings—particularly the larger pilings—serves as a resting area for fish that can still watch for passing food.

It pays to explore pilings. Most bridges have a number of pilings, with some of these always producing fish and some never producing fish. Fish all the pilings several times under different circumstances to find out which pilings are best. Cast all around larger pilings and pay particular attention to the down-tide side, which provides the maximum buffer water.

Dock and Piers

Docks and piers serve the same purpose in the fish world as do bridge pilings. Fish them the same way, casting all around each piling and noting for future reference those which are best. In saltwater fishing, the buffer area for a piling or pier where most fish cluster, varies with

READING SALTWATER

Large pilings, such as this structure for the Chesapeake Bay Bridge in Maryland, are ideal for holding saltwater fish such as stripers, bluefish, seatrout, etc. Fish these carefully, taking care to work the changing tides for best results.

each tide change. Hit these on a running tide, concentrating on the buffer, down-tide area.

Jetties

Simply man-made rock shorelines, jetties stick out into the ocean to hold sand or stabilize shorelines. Fish them like any rocky area, casting parallel to the rock when drifting close, or casting at right angles to the jetty from slightly offshore.

Breakwaters

Breakwater can be another word for jetty, but is often a solid concrete wall to protect an area. As such, they have less surface area; fewer nooks and crannies for algae, mussels and baitfish; and no protected areas or pockets for these or for gamefish. Breakwaters are less likely to be good spots to fish than jetties and rip rap, but are worth a try if they create water protected from tidal currents or tend to hold bait that winds or tides push to that shore.

Flotsam

A dictionary definition of flotsam is any man-made wreckage or debris, especially from a wrecked ship. From the fly fisher's standpoint, it can also include debris from anywhere–natural materials such as dislodged trees, weeds and patches of floating grass. These are ideal for both coastal and pelagic fish, since flotsam serves as shade, attracts bait and thus attracts gamefish from stripers to dolphin. When encountered, flotsam is always worth a cast or two.

Oil Rigs

Offshore oil rigs are private property. Don't tie up to them. They are prime areas—primarily in the Gulf of Mexico where they are prevalent—for everything from sharks to cobia to grouper. Fish them from the down-current side. That way you can hold your boat in position without risking it drifting into the rig. Use polarizing glasses to scope the water around and under the rig so that you avoid any wires, struts, posts or other obstructions. The best safe fishing is just to the edge of the oil rig to attract fish that are hanging around the periphery.

Channel Markers

Fish will hold around channel markers, but you can't tie up to them and you must be ready to give way to any moving boat. These are often good places for stripers and sea trout, sometimes cobia. Fish the down current side of the piling or post, but be ready to move out of the way of boats moving through the channel.

Buoys

You can't tie up to any buoy either, but these are often ideal spots for cobia in southern Atlantic coast waters. Fish from the down current/down tide side so that you can hold the boat in place. If this spot is also downwind, realize that you will be casting into the wind to reach the area around the buoy.

Artificial Reefs

Artificial reefs have been constructed in areas where natural reefs have been destroyed, or where natural structure is absent, such as the south Atlantic coast. They have been made of everything, including trolley cars, autos, train cars, buses, construction rubble, special molded concrete shapes, weighted tires and old ships. That they attract and hold fish is without question, although some are better than others, due to construction and geography. The main problem with artificial reefs is that many of them are too deep for effective fly fishing, and if shallow, can catch flies to make fishing difficult. You will find most marked with buoys indicating their outermost limits; you will also find artificial reefs indicated on nautical charts.

Chapter 7

Presenting the Fly—Practical Approaches and Techniques

Making short casts and then lengthening them while working downstream one or two steps at a time makes it easy to cover big water on a larger river when trout or salmon fishing.

Each type of water and species of fish has its own best ways of approach, casting, fishing, presenting the fly and convincing a fish that what you are offering is something good to eat. Here are some general ways to approach fly fishing in many situations.

You should have a plan before you make the first cast. Stand back and study the water to figure out the best approach to take. In some cases, this might be self-evident. If you are wading a big smallmouth river, often the best approach is to fan cast your way across the river, or work upstream to hit rocks and riffles, working to the right and left as you go to cover all the possible water in your immediate casting range.

If sight fishing a flat, it helps to search ahead to figure out the best possible approach (boat fishing or wading) to cover the water. Or, if you see a distant pod of bonefish, you can plan on the best possible way to intersect them to make the best possible cast. If fishing a trout stream, effective fishing often requires figuring out casts, possible approaches, positions for getting a drag-free drift, choosing the right fly and possible locations of the best trout in a pool before making the first cast.

Just because you can cast a long distance, it's not always your best option—at least at first. Often this will line a closer fish and destroy the chances for taking that fish. In a worst case scenario, the fish that you line will blow off and in turn scare the fish you were watching or those in the holding spot that you were initially aiming for.

Even if you don't see any nearby fish, it pays to make short casts first to all likely spots, gradually increasing the length of the cast and the range that you fish until you can reach the spot that you picked as the prime target. A basic technique for Atlantic salmon fishing is to position yourself in the water (or the guides will hold you in position in a canoe) then make short casts and allow each cast to drift and swing in the current. Then increase each cast by at least a foot (30.5 cm) of line until you have reached the maximum effective casting range. Continue to cast at that range while working downstream.

Long Pools

The step-down method of fishing long pools is to cover all the water thoroughly. It is a common and established method for fishing Atlantic salmon, but will work on any fish in any running water that has long, large pools. It follows the fishing method above of fishing close and then gradually extending the cast. The above method brackets and completely covers the water when fishing in one spot by allowing the fly to swing with the current from the cross-stream cast to straight downstream.

To cover a large pool, make one or two steps downstream after the longest cast that you can reasonably make. Repeat this long cast to allow the fly to drift through water just slightly downstream of the previous cast. By repeating this, with a step or two between each cast, you can cover the entire pool. Naturally, this assumes a relatively even pool or glide with few exposed rocks around which you would have to cast, or deep shoreline holes that would be impossible to wade. It is a good, thorough method for fishing any long pool using one pattern of fly. Once you complete this, you can move back up to the head of the pool and repeat this with a different fly or move on to the next pool.

Shad fishing for hickory shad or the larger American shad is simple, and only requires getting to the best spot in the river to snake a fly through the tail of a pool to catch fish that are ascending streams in their migratory spawning runs.

Proper boat handling (or canoe handling in this case) is a must to be able to position a cast away from the shore or weed beds to take largemouth like this one.

A low rod and somewhat crouched position is ideal when sight fishing or when expecting a strike. This allows immediate contact with the fish.

PRESENTING THE FLY

Boat Fishing

When boat-fishing a shore-line, you only have to figure out the best approach (right to left or left to right) to cover the shore. There are several ways to move along a shore, with your fishing buddy or the guide working a push pole, an electric motor, paddle or allowing the wind to drift you along. Seldom will the wind exactly parallel the shore, though this is nice when it does happen. Make all casts at right angles to the boat to avoid casting axial to the boat and risk hitting a companion, guide or boat structure. When two or more anglers are in the boat, it helps to take turns casting to avoid accidents. If by chance one of you is right-handed and the other left-handed, take bow and stern positions so that the casting arm is outboard to avoid casting over the boat.

In any casting situation, keep the boat the maximum casting distance away from the shore to prevent spooking fish. Keeping the boat a set distance from the shore, makes it easier to maintain a good, accurate cast each time.

To hold the line, use a stripping basket to keep the line from blowing around on a boat deck or from drifting in the water when wading or shore fishing. Stripping baskets for wading are available in many styles—from punctured (to let water out) plastic washbasins to cloth baskets in wire frames. The best baskets today fit to the side of you, since stripping line in involves pulling line to your line hand side—not in front of you. You can buy

commercial stand-alone baskets for boats, but a functional alternative is either a tall mesh laundry hamper or one of the spring-style laundry baskets or leaf buckets sold in general stores. Another boat alternative is to lay a square of artificial turf on a boat deck to secure the line.

Swing Fly in Current

This is a trick of allowing a fly to swing through the current until it is straight downstream, then swinging the fly back and forth to coax hits. It works for any fish that holds in the tail of pools, especially spawning fish such as steelhead, shad, salmon and the like. To do this, work the fly straight downstream, then flip

the rod to one side, holding the tip low. The current catches the belly of the line and pushes it downstream in an arc to flip the fly to one side as the line straightens out. Then flip the rod to the other side to repeat this and cause the fly to flip back the other way. You can do this as long as you like, but a second cast is best after a few flips back and forth with no hit.

Fishing Through Weed Beds

Weeds hold fish, but are tough to fish in. Weeds also create problems with getting a line, leader and fly through them to fish effectively. Here are some tips for fishing weeds:

- Knots catch weeds. In any weed situation, try to use a

It's important to have a good guide and poler, such as Capt. John Kumiski here, poling Brenda Pfeiffer on the east coast of Florida for redfish. Poling is valuable to keep the angler a set distance from the target area to make casting easier.

Steelhead like this one caught by Jim Heim are easily taken on the fly, but require heavily weighted flies or leaders to get the bright flies or glo bugs deep in the riffles to where the fish will see and take them.

knotless or level leader. You can't make a tapered knotless leader, but they are available in shops. An easy alternative for most fish is to use a long level leader that you can run from the loop at the fly line to the knot on the fly. Since most fish will be fairly large in this fishing and weeds will hide the leader anyway, try to get by with the heaviest possible leader. Weeds are typical habitat for bass, pike, musky, redfish, sea trout and others, so a leader of 15- to 20-pound-test (6.8- to 9.1-kg) is a good start.

- Use a weedless fly. The best is the double loop mono weedguard, although wire prong weedguards [braided wire 30-pound test (13.6-kg) for size 2 and under flies; 40-pound test (18.1-kg) for size 1 and larger flies] are best when fishing for toothy fish such as pike, musky or barracuda. Toothy fish cut mono weedguards, while the braided wire weedguards will hold up and can be re-bent to shape if deformed during the fight.
- If the weeds are underwater, use a floating line or sinking tip line that will keep the main body of the line above the weeds. You will catch fewer weeds this way and can pick up the line easier.
- If the weeds are on the top, use a slow (sink rate of 1— or sinking about 1/2 to 11/2 inches/2.5 to 3.8 cm per second) full sinking line. This will allow you to get under the weeds and get a good retrieve. A tip here is to make up (from an old scrap floating fly line) some short lengths of a mini floating head—about 5 feet (1.5 m) of floating line with loops spliced on each end. Attach this between the line and leader to float the leader and fly some to keep them at the upper part of the water column. This is the reverse of using mini lead heads to sink a fly when using a floating line.

Fishing Deep

Use the count-down method only for retrieved flies—not those fished in a dead drift, where it won't matter anyway. Don't use it with a sinking-tip line, since the floating main part of the line will tend to plane up the fly during the retrieve. Use this with a full sinking line on a long cast. As the fly starts to sink, count in seconds ("one-thousand-one, one-thousand-two. . .") until you reach the depth desired and then begin the retrieve. Hold the rod tip down or even underwater to keep the fly at the same depth throughout the retrieve. Try different depths until you get a strike and then fish at that depth repeatedly.

Fishing Floating Flies

If fishing on the bottom in relatively shallow water, it often helps to keep the fly just a little above the bottom to attract fish. To do this, use a floating fly with a short leader (about 3 feet/1 m) on a full fast sinking line. The line might scrape, but the floating fly will stay above the bottom. If lacking a suitable floating fly, use a foam strike indicator about 12 inches (30.5 cm) ahead of the fly to keep it up.

Fishing Sinking Flies

You can control the depth of a fly by fishing a sinking fly with a floating line. This means not just any fly (they all sink except those specifically designed to float—like dry flies, cork and foam popping bugs and deer hair bugs) but one with a little weight built into the fly. For this, you want a fly with only a little weight, since too much weight will pull the fly line down and sink the fly below the depth you desire.

Weight with Mini Lead Heads

In addition to using the sinking leaders that are now available, you can also use mini lead heads that are available from several companies (Gudebrod, Orvis, Cortland). These come in various lengths and are easy to loop between your fly line and leader to help sink a line. They are also ideal for use with sinking and sinking tip lines, as they help to sink a leader and fly to get it to the desired depth in the water column.

Casting onto Land

One way to fool fish when shoreline fishing is to cast your weedless fly onto the shore (about a foot/30.5 cm), then snake the fly out into the water. Depending upon the fish sought and the type of fly you use, the fish might think that this is an insect, lizard, caterpillar, worm, mouse or frog. Often this is a better approach than dropping the fly onto the water, particularly in very skinny shallows where fish easily spook. This is a good bass technique, but will work for other species.

Hitting Structure for Effect

When you hit a structure on purpose, it tends to wake up a fish. It is a good bass fishing technique, throwing a floating bug with a side cast so that you hit a stump, duck blind, standing timber, piling or abandoned boat. Just make sure that you don't do this on private property and that you plan this to hit solid structure to prevent getting hung up in a brush pile. The knock often piques the curiosity of fish while the bug dropping into the water imitates an injured insect.

Anglers often mistake a "tailing" fish for a feeding rise. In all likelihood, these fish are rooting for immature insects or other foods on the bottom of the stream. Trout behaving this way aren't likely to take a dry fly; you should fish using subsurface techniques instead.

Fish Sign

Fish sometimes signal their presence by various signs that are easy to detect once you know what to look for. These include:

Nervous Water

Nervous water is a term used to indicate bait close to the top of the water—there as a result of gamefish that are pushing them up. Do not run the boat through schools like this (it puts them down) and stay a cast length away to fish the edge of the school. In deep water, this can change instantly into breaking fish with bait exploding everywhere as gamefish crash bait. You will typically find this in saltwater situations, but can also find it with largemouth and smallmouth bass.

Finning or Tailing Fish

Fish that have their dorsal fins or tails out of the water are in skinny water. The exception to that are sharks which do swim the surface with fins and sometimes tail out. In open water, sharks going in a straight line are probably not too interested in gulping a fly, while those that are swimming in random patterns may be looking for baitfish and ready to take a fly.

On skinny flats, you can find finning and tailing sharks, tarpon, permit and bonefish. In coastal shoal areas, redfish act the same way. If fish are on a flat or shallow slough, they are interested in eating. How these

A type of subtle rise, called slipping rise, generally indicates that fish are leisurely feeding on flies resting on the surface of the water. As the trout sucks in an insect, it creates a series of concentric rings. Sipping rises are difficult to spot in rough water. Trout feeding in sips are vulnerable to an adult fly imitation cast well ahead of the rise, provided the fly resembles the actual insects being eaten.

Head-and-tail rise usually means the trout is feeding on insects stuck in the surface film. The trout's head appears first, then the dorsal fin and tail are visible as the fish rolls. An angler often gets results by presenting a fly that resembles a terrestrial, an emerging aquaqtic insect or a spent adult insect. The best presentation is to cast the fly up-current from the trout's last rise and let it drift naturally past the lie.

fish react indicates how or even if they might eat a fly. Those that are moving in a straight line or larger zigzags might be feeding or might be just cruising, looking for food. Bonefish often stop to root around on the bottom for urchins, crabs, shrimp and anything else that they can find to eat. When doing this they can "mud" an area, creating puffs of mud that are indicative of actively feeding fish. Seeing any activity like this is golden, since it is a sure mark of fish in the area and fish eating.

Nymph-Seeking Trout

Trout often grub along on the bottom, working through and around rocks to dislodge and eat nymphs of mayflies, caddis flies and stoneflies. Hellgrammites and the larva of damselflies and dragonflies are also targets. These fish can sometimes be spotted by their action of moving to the side to dislodge nymphs—an action that exposes their bellies. A flash of white deep in a pool indicates trout feeding this way. Sometimes you can also spot trout taking nymphs by spotting their open white mouth as they gulp flies.

Rising Fish

Trout, as well as other fish, rise to the surface to take maturing insects. Sunfish and bass will take insects and bass will also take frogs, mice and voles. Pike will take baby ducks and small mammals off of the surface. We don't think of these as rises, but they are surface activities. Carp will cruise the surface taking seed and insects. All are indications of active feeding, but require matching the hatch to what the fish want.

Spawning Fish

Flashes in the water similar to trout dislodging underwater nymphs can indicate spawning fish. This is typical during spring and fall spawning runs (which vary with different species) but makes for a very difficult time to take fish. Some fish, such as trout, do become aggressive and will hit and chase away anything in their territory. Bass will do the same thing to protect their nests and eggs. As a result of this protective action, some anglers feel that it is unsporting to take spawning fish that are trying to protect eggs and young.

Migrating Fish

You can spot migrating fish in several ways. One of the best

When making long casts, never let go of the line, since this does not allow accuracy and also might miss a fish if one hits at the end of the cast. Instead, as the author is doing here, allow the line to run through the line hand to maintain constant control.

in shallow rivers is watching for the thrashing and splashing that they make as they move upriver. This is typical for both American and hickory shad. You can spot steelhead and salmon (particularly Pacific salmon) pushing upstream often like miniature submarines pushing water and making a wake without actually splashing or finning.

Smell

Large schools of fish sometimes leave a smell. This is particularly true of bluefish, which leave a smell like cucumbers. Local conditions and fish prey may dictate this with other fish in certain areas.

Oil Slicks

Bluefish will also leave an oil slick when they are chopping up and feeding on the oily menhaden—a favorite coastal food of big gamefish. This oil slick might be a precursor of action to come—or it could mean you should have been there earlier when the fish were feeding.

Water Color

Large, close masses of fish will darken the water from their collective bodies. You can find different colors, depending upon the fish species. The color depends not only on the fish, but also the color of the bottom and the water for a given area, so local knowledge is vital to use this information. In west coast streams, you can also see salmon in their pink and red stages as they ascend streams.

Birds

Birds can be the bird dogs for fly fishing. Birds working over bait are most prevalent in saltwater, but you can also find gulls working over shad pushed to the surface by largemouth bass. In all cases, the actions of birds will indicate fishing possibilities For example:

- Large flocks of birds sitting on the water may mean that there is deep bait and that the birds are just waiting for the bait to push to the surface.
- Birds flying from one spot to another means nothing—they are moving, not concentrating on bait.
- Birds that are hovering over a spot are usually waiting for feeding fish to push bait to the top. Stick around for the action.
- Birds actively diving are taking bait that fish miss or chop up, typically stripers and bluefish. Get in on the action.

On big water, long casts are often the best way to fish, starting with a short cast, then lengthening the cast and working downstream to cover new water with each swing of the fly on each cast.

Chapter 8

Tactics for Freshwater Fish—Trout, Bass, Pike, Carp, Crappie, Sunfish

Long pools are best fished carefully and slowly with a slow natural drift of the fly through the main part of the pool.

Every fish species has unique habits and special habitats. Here are some tips and tricks to take a variety of popular freshwater fish.

Trout

You'll find trout (and salmon) in streams, rivers, ponds and lakes. Lake fishing is mostly hardware fishing by trolling and is not as important to the fly angler. It can be good, particularly along the shore when the trout are entering streams to spawn. It can also be good when trout are holding in weed beds. The best technique is to fish nymphs or streamers, although dry fly fishing can be excellent when the fish are taking insects off the surface.

Most trout fishing is stream fishing, be that stream tiny or large. Here the constant water flow makes for both an advantage and disadvantage for fly fishing. How you use the water can determine your success of the day.

Pond fishing is different, in that trout are more widely scattered than would be bass or sunfish in a similar situation. To fish ponds for trout, you need to do much exploring to find the right spot, or you can fish the pond in sequential steps and areas to explore all the water with a fly.

Tackle Tactics

One way to get more trout is to use the lightest possible tackle. Many anglers use 6- or 7-weight outfits when a 3- or 4-weight would be far better. If you are not casting big flies, consider a 1- or 2-weight. The lighter the outfit you have, the lighter the fall on the water of the line, leader and fly. That reduces the possibility that the line will scare the trout. This will not work, or work well, if you are casting large streamers, Muddlers or Clousers, since they require a larger line to turn over the fly.

For casting small flies with only an occasional foray with big flies, stick with the small outfit. To compensate for the larger flies, shorten the leader for an easier turnover, use more

---

Suggested Outfits for Trout Fly Size

Rod/Line Weight	Fly Sizes
1	#26 to #16
2	#22 to #14
3	#20 to #10
4	#16 to #8 or #6
5	#12 to #6 or #4
6	#10 to #2

Note that you can always cast smaller flies than those listed. The above listing could have had size #26 as the smallest in each of the categories.

Note also that the above does not take into account the differences in flies. You won't be able to cast weighted or very bulky flies in these size ranges, while you can cast some flies outside of these ranges. You can always cast smaller flies, even though the outfit might be heavier than required for that fly.

---

force in the cast and keep the loop narrow to push out the fly.

The lighter outfit works fine for most trout fishing and also gives you more excitement in fighting the fish.

Leader Length

Adjust your leader length based on the water fished. Trout are spooky, but on a small mountain stream with lots of foam, plunge pools, riffles and rapids, a short leader of 7$\frac{1}{2}$ feet (2.3 m) should work well. You can adjust leader length for trout based on the water fished. On these streams, most fishing is with very short line—and little of the line or even the leader reaches the water.

Use longer leaders on larger streams and ponds, based in part on water clarity and also

One way to sneak up on trout is to camouflage your fly line by marking it with permanent markers.

Tippet Size

You must gear tippet size to the size of the fly and also to the size of the trout. Too light a tippet can collapse with bulky or weighted flies, while too heavy a leader can spook trout. Note that longer tippets are best for spooky trout to separate them from the line and rest of the leader. Some suggestions for fly size and tippet size are:

Tippet Size	Approximate Pound-Test	Fly Size
8X	0.75 to 1 (0.3 to 0.5 kg)	#28 to #20
7X	1 to 2 (0.5 to 0.9 kg)	#24 to #18
6X	1.5 to 2 (0.7 to 0.9 kg)	#22 to #16
5X	2.5 to 3 (1.1 to 1.4 kg)	#20 to #14
4X	3 to 4 (1.4 to 1.8 kg)	#16 to #10
3X	4 to 5 (1.8 to 2.3 kg)	#12 to #6
2X	5 to 6 (2.3 to 2.7 kg)	#10 to #2
1X	6 to 7 (2.7 to 3.2 kg)	#8 to #1

the amount of open water where the trout can examine the fly. On these waters, go with a minimum or 9 feet (2.7 m) of leader, and use leaders up to 15 feet (4.6 m) on very clear water. Longer tippets are also good for this fishing, since they separate the thicker parts of the leader from the trout, and also allow for more movement of the fly, along with stack or pile casting for a natural drift.

Approach Strategy

Avoid having anything shiny that can cause specular highlights in the sun and alert trout to your presence. Keep fly dressing bottles, hemostats, nippers and other necessary tools in your pockets. Avoid using reels with shiny finishes. If possible, choose rods with a matte finish or rub your rod lightly with fine steel wool to remove any gloss finish that might scare trout. Before you reach the river, dull

the shiny finish on your leader twist-on lead sheets by dipping them in vinegar.

Dress appropriately. Clothing that matches the background—even camouflage clothing—is best for serious stream or river trout fishing. If you can't find a camouflage vest, wear a light-weight oversize camouflage shirt over your vest to disguise it. Wear a brimmed cap with a dark underbrim to prevent light from bouncing into your eyes. Use polarized sunglasses to reduce glare.

Have your tackle ready when you approach the stream, river or pond. If you're pond fishing from a boat or canoe, do not take along rod cases or other gear—leave that in the car. Be ready to fish, with the exception of tying on the fly. The reason for this is that the water will tell you what fly to fish. On a stream, you might find a particular hatch occurring when you get to the water, or

low/high water conditions might dictate a particular tactics of going small (low water) or fishing deep (high water).

More fish are "lost" before we even get to the water than we will ever know. Trout are keenly aware of their surroundings and any slight changes in their environment. Stay back from the stream to watch it for a while, hiding where possible.

The refraction of light through the water allows a trout to see through its "window" anything that is above an angle of about 10 degrees above the water surface.

If you are 40 feet (12.2 m) away, you can stand; if you are 20 feet (6.1 m) away, kneel to stay completely hidden. For small stream trout fishing, invest in knee pads for comfort and to avoid wader wear—you will catch more fish.

Even though you are wearing waders or hip boots, do not

enter the water unless absolutely necessary. Stay back and blend in with the background. If you must enter the water, wade very slowly. If you see waves or water pressure rings being pushed in front of you, the trout can also feel this on their lateral line. This is more important than any noise that you might make crunching along the bottom. If you wade, wade sideways to the current so that you present less water resistance to the current and less possibility of creating pressure waves.

Plan your approach to and through the water. On small streams, this usually means working upstream so that the trout can't see your approach. Keep to one side of the stream so that you can make casts that are angled upstream to prevent straight upstream casts that line the trout.

Look for a different approach. If there is a trail along one side of the stream, consider possible approaches from the opposite side. Ninety-nine percent of anglers fish from the trail side, but this assures that trout see flies presented only from that side. An approach and fly presentation from the opposite side can produce more trout.

Check the water for trout sign before you get to the banks. Check for rises that indicate hatches or trout taking egg laying spinners from the surface. Look underneath the water for flashes of bellies, mouths or fins as trout work on the rocks and gravel to take nymphs. Look for currents by following foam and other detritus floating downstream, to figure the feeding lanes and your necessary cast to get a drag-free float through these areas.

Hit the Holding Areas

Structure fills trout streams—rocks, boulders, cliffs, downed trees, rip rap, weed beds, riffles, rapids and plunge pools. All of these provide the buffer areas for trout to rest in and are prime targets. How you approach them is the key to taking trout—lots of trout.

There are two ways to work structure, and each has its advantages. One way is to start at the tail end of a pool or selected area and work upstream, planning your attack to hit each of the possible trout lies as you progress. The

Cross-stream casts (left) are often best with a little bit of slack in them to allow the current to wash out the slack while the fly gets a natural drift.

The choice of upstream or downstream casts (above) is one that is important in fly fishing streams. Usually dry fly fishing is upstream and wet fly and nymph fishing is downstream.

second is to start with the least good-looking spot, knowing that any trout there are among the smallest of the pool. You can take the smallest trout first, and then work your way to the next possible spot and on to the best spot in the stream, which should hold the largest trout. The only problem is that we are people, not trout, so we can't always determine the best spot or succession of good spots from the trout's standpoint.

Work Upstream When Dry Fly Fishing

The best way to approach trout in a river or stream is to work upstream. This allows approaching the trout from behind and also allows upstream casts with a dry fly to take trout with the best possible chances of a drag-free float. It also allows fishing a wet fly or nymph, if inclined, as you work your way upstream. One easy way to do this without retying flies all the time is to pretie a nymph or wet fly to a leader tippet and use a loop knot to connect the fly/tippet to the rest of the leader. Do this also with the dry that you select. Disconnect and reconnect loops to change flies as you fish to switch back and forth between flies.

Dapping with Nymphs

Since trout take more of their food on the bottom, the best way to take lots of trout is to fish there. Since trout can take in and spit out a nymph before we know it, the best way to fish is by dapping. For this, use a 9-foot (2.7 m) rod, weighted nymph and approach stealthily. Drop the fly into the

water using a very short length of line so that little leader touches the water and the fly drifts freely from the vertically dropped leader tippet. With the slightest touch or slowing of the fly, strike.

Nymph fishing with strike indicators is a second way to nymph fish. This allows traditional casting and a longer line to reach spots that are more distant. Carry several different colors of strike indicator. Wool yarn is perhaps best and easiest to use. For maximum visibility, use black yarn when there is a lot of glare on the water. Chartreuse is also a good color for many situations. If the strike indicator stops, slows or disappears, strike.

Pick the Right Cast

Knowing different casts for trout fishing (such as Lazy-S, pile or tuck), still requires that you know when to use each cast. For casting across currents, the lazy-S cast is best. For getting a weighted nymph into the water and sinking rapidly, use the forceful tuck cast. For a slow natural drift of a fly in an eddy or small pocket of water, use the pile cast to provide extra tippet and slack for the fly.

Pond Fishing

If fishing for pond trout from a boat or canoe, use scrap carpeting in the bottom to prevent sound that can transmit through the bottom and scare trout. In canoes, slip some pipe insulation along the gunwales to prevent paddles knocking the craft and making noise. Plan your approach with the canoe or boat so that you can hit spots around the pond in a logical sequence.

Bass

Bass are structure oriented. Largemouth like wood structures and smallmouth like rock, but both species will utilize any available structure. Learn the structure in your fishing areas and concentrate on fishing those areas and those areas alone. Note that structure in this case means not only rip rap, gravel bars, boulders, stumps, log jams and downed trees, but also lily pads, breakline areas and grass beds. Stay away from open water and fish any structure you find.

Fishing Structure

Cast short to structure before zeroing in on the target. More than one bass can hang around any given structure, but the best bass take the closest and best spot. To get more than one bass from a structure, cast short and fan cast around the area. Make each successive cast closer to the structure target until you bracket that area several times to attract bass.

Fish a weedless fly or bug and throw it right at a piece of structure, hitting it if you are sure that it can't snag. This slight "knock" can wake up bass and provoke a hit. A good technique for this is to hit the structure (such as a stump or standing tree) above the waterline and let the bug/fly fall into the water. Allow is to lay there as if stunned before twitching it—but be prepared for a strike as soon as the fly moves.

On cloudy or overcast days, bass are more likely to cruise than hold close to structure as they do on sunny days. For this, fish structure, but make casts that are farther away from the structure. Cloudy days are often a time when smallmouth bass form feeding lanes (almost like trout) in rivers to take emerging nymphs.

On bright days, bass hold to the shady side of any surface structure. This can include the shady side of standing timber, docks, piers, bridge pilings, stumps and boathouses. Bass stay beneath the shady lily pads and spatterdock. Try these spots first.

Breaklines For Bass

You'll find great fly-fishing for bass along breaklines. These are areas that parallel the shore, following the shore's curvature, where the lake bottom drops off sharply from the shallow sloping shore. You can't read these from the surface, but you can find them with a depth finder. Bass and other fish hang out along spots like this, particularly during hot summer months.

Bass come up into the shallows from the breakline dropoffs in the early morning and in the late evening, providing more traditional surface or shallow fishing. In trout lakes, you'll find trout cruising along these deep areas, but seldom moving into the shallows, as do bass.

Bass (left) are often caught around weeds and will dive into them after being hooked, which is why this bass leader has a lot of grass hanging from it. This largemouth was taken on a white popper in a Texas pond.

Sneaking a fly through gaps in lily pads (above) or other surface weeds is one way to get into weed beds and still get bass.

Simple poppers and an 8-weight outfit make it possible to get in on a lot of bass fishing, such as this nice catch of a largemouth by King Montgomery.

Casting nymphs upstream (below) is a great way to fish for both trout and smallmouth bass, but it requires careful attention to the line to keep slack out while not retrieving the fly, to allow the fly a natural drift.

TACTICS FOR FRESHWATER FISH

Pike

Pike, pickerel and musky typically hang out in weed beds. Most of these weed beds in the North Country are long grass, often bent by current or wind in one direction. The wrong way to fish these is at right angles to the wind or current. Even with a weedless fly, you end up dragging the fly through the weeds, sometimes cutting them and usually scaring more fish than you catch. The right way to fish such weeds is to pick one of two methods:

- Work the edge of the weed bed, fishing the edges by casting close to and parallel to the edge of the weeds. Often pike will hang in these areas to ambush prey. A fly fished this way can take big pike. An added advantage is that often it is easy to coax the pike into the open water where they are easier to fight, less likely to get tangled in the weeds and less likely to scare any other pike that might be in the weeds.

- Try fishing the weeds after working and thoroughly fishing the weed edges. For this, position the boat so that you are casting in line with the direction of the weeds. Usually this is directly with or against any wind or current that will push the weeds. This allows snaking the fly through the weeds without cutting them or snagging a weed stalk.

One way to land pike so that they can easily be released is to use a wide cradle, rather than a net. The cradle picks up the fish carefully and allows hook removal so the pike can be lowered into the water and released.

Sinking Line

Pike fishing is often on big water. That means chop and waves on the surface, which means that a slow sinking line is better than a floating line, even if using a top water popper. The slow sinking line (sink rate of $1/2$ to $1 1/2$ inches/1.3 to 3.8 cm per second) will shed any grass that might be floating on the surface and also keep a straight line with the retrieved fly to prevent slack in the line as might occur as a floating line bobs on the surface. If you need to fish deep, then go with a faster sinking line.

Big Flies

Fish such as perch, suckers, sauger and trout are favorite pike meals, so you need a large streamer fly that will resemble one of these favorite foods. You also need to fish it right. This means a retrieve that consists of long strips of the fly, pause, short twitches and so on. Think like a nervous baitfish and make your fly act accordingly.

Poppers

Surface strikes from pike are not quite as explosive as those from saltwater fish, but they are hard and vicious. Big poppers are a must for this. I like those that have foam with long synthetic tails that will hold up to the teeth a little longer than cork and feathers. Best colors are black and white, red and yellow, all yellow and brown and yellow. These colors simulate the colors of perch, sauger, walleye and similar pike food fish.

Best pike fishing (above) is fishing around weed beds and grass with a big fly that will simulate a sucker or perch or other baitfish native to the water.

This pike (right) was taken on a large fly that simulates a large baitfish. Large flies are often necessary for large fish, since a large single meal is preferred over several smaller meals by most fish.

TACTICS FOR FRESHWATER FISH

Carp

Carp are mostly bottom feeders. Best fishing in a known carp area is with crayfish imitations or Clouser minnows, fished and twitched slowly right on the bottom. Use the count down method and a full sinking line to get rapidly to the fish and stay there. Usually this is only good if you see "muds" through the water where the carp are feeding. Otherwise, this is merely a long, slow painful exercise in blind fishing.

Carp will cruise the shallows in lake or rivers. This is just like freshwater bonefish, where you have to be stealthy, plan your approach and make long accurate casts and plan the target area to be just in front of the moving carp. It is not always easy. The best approach—as with any fish—is from the rear of the moving carp and off to the side, casting to drop the fly so that the twitches of the fly and the movement of the carp will intersect. Wait for the carp to take the fly and you feel the weight before striking. Best flies are any bottom flies including Clouser minnows, crayfish imitations, weighted woolly buggers and sinking Muddler minnows.

Follow Smallmouth

Where carp and smallmouth are found in the same waters, they often feed together. Clousers or other bottom-fished flies are ideal for this. It is almost like sight fishing for bonefish. The technique is to work the boat through shallows (a push pole is best for this, operated from the rear of the boat), then cast ahead when you see carp, dropping the fly in their feeding path and working it in short twitches. To avoid lining the fish, work from the side and rear and cast ahead of them. If the twitched flies spook carp, try casting and letting the carp move right over the fly or as close as you expect them to move. Then make a slight twitch as if the crayfish is trying to get away. Often carp will suck up a fly fished this way. The one disadvantage of this is that often a smallmouth will run forward and grab the fly before the carp has a chance.

Small Flies on Top

During the summer, carp cruise the surface of large waterways to take insects and seeds off the surface. The fishing is just like that for bonefish, except on top of a lake instead of on the bottom of a tropical flat. Insects can include mayflies, caddis, stoneflies and midges. Plant food can include seeds of cottonwood, thistle, dandelion and milkweed. This technique is usually only best when there are lots of seeds or insects on the surface, often in late spring or mid-summer. At this time, you will likely find large schools of carp cruising the surface, feeding in a random pattern. There are two ways to capitalize on this:

- With insects on the surface, fish standard dry flies. Go with as small as you think can hold the fish, and as large as you think the carp will take. Often this can be a size 12 or 14 fly, unless they are taking midges, in which case try to get some hits from a size 16. Depending upon the size of the carp, the larger the fly, the fewer the hits (the less likely it will match the natural), but the more likely you will land the fish or at least keep it on for a while.

- If the carp are taking plant seeds, fish a size 16 or 14 white CDC or marabou fluff fly that will closely imitate dandelion or cottonwood seeds. You can also fish midges in larger sizes to imitate thistle seeds.

In all cases, lighten the drag on the reel as much as possible, since with any decent size fish, just pulling the line around will be enough drag. Anything more will risk bending the fly hook. The best technique is to follow the movements of the carp, approach stealthily, make long casts in front of the fish and wait for a hit.

Mulberry Fishing

The fact that carp like plant food is also evidenced by the fact that they will hang out around shore-growing mulberry trees to take the mulberries that fall into the water each summer. This will vary with latitude, but in the mid-Atlantic it occurs around mid-July. Since the mulberries "plop" into the water, a careful cast is not necessary, even though a stealthy approach is still best. Try flies that are nothing more than clipped red or purple deer hair tied onto a hook, or a 1/2-inch (1.3-cm) pom pom (check your local craft store) glued to a large fly hook. Carry a few of both types of flies, since the deer-hair flies will float while the pom-pom flies will slowly sink, but will soak up water in time.

Crappie

Crappies eat lots of small minnows. The best flies for them are small weedless streamers, thrown right into crappie havens, such as brush piles or around bridge pilings. Best size flies are those from about size 10 to size 6, with yellow a good wing or body color choice.

Weedless Flies

If you find crappie around brush piles, you will need weedless flies. The best flies are those with a single mono weedguard that will shed most brush. Best flies will have both a weedguard and a little weight, such as a small dumbbell eye or a metal cone head or bead to help sink it. Cast right into a brush pile, let the fly sink and then snake it out slowly with short twitches that will imitate minnow-like darting action. This fishing is best in the spring and fall.

Structure Fishing

One of the best ways to fish crappie in the summer is to fish with a sinking line, short leader and sinking fly to fish around pilings, bridge supports, docks, piers and the like. In the summer, crappie tend to go deep. Use streamer flies or woolly buggers to imitate minnows.

Rocky bottoms often hold crappies in the spring. The rocks absorb sunlight and warm the surrounding water, attracting baitfish and other crappie food.

Brush piles—natural or man-made—are excellent crappie producers, especially if they stand several feet (meters) above the bottom and have many openings between the branches.

Bluegills—along with other sunfish—are a lot of fun on light outfits that can cast wet flies and tiny popping bugs.

Sunfish

Sunfish, like bass, make beds for spawning. Both are in close to shore, both are circular and both species protect their young. To fish for sunfish in the spring, use small bright underwater wet flies. Weighted flies are best to sink rapidly to the beds where sunfish will eagerly take them.

Poppers

Sunfish have small mouths, so buy or tie bugs with a small long shank hook. Best are poppers and sliders that are small with a long shank hook for easy unhooking. The best poppers should be no more than 1/4 inch (6 mm) in diameter.

Terrestrials

Sunfish often take small hoppers, ants, beetles, leafhoppers and such. Fish these imitations in both surface and underwater styles. Use a dead drift or slow, even retrieve for the underwater flies and tiny twitches with surface bugs.

Tandem Fly Rigs

Sunfish travel in schools, so one fish usually means a lot of fish. To make the most of this, use tandem rigs with a sinking wet fly tied 18 inches (45.7 cm) from a small popper. Use the same mono as the tippet and knot the leader to the bend of the popper hook. Fish the popper and allow the wet fly to hang in the water. Don't be surprised if a sunfish hits the fly after another takes the popper. This is also a great way to take sunfish when they are reluctant to take a popper. The popper serves to make a little noise to wake up the fish and also serves as a bobber to float the tandem fly at a predetermined (by the tandem leader length) depth.

Chapter 9

Tactics for Saltwater Fish—Inshore, Offshore, Tropical

Commercial trawling boats often work up bait and bottom material to attract both gamefish and birds. These birds are a good indication of bait in the area, and also a good indication that gamefish are under the bait.

You can translate many of the methods used in freshwater to saltwater, but there are also special tactics that are unique to the salt.

Inshore and Coastal Saltwater Tactics

Tides and other saltwater fishing conditions require totally different ways of thinking about saltwater fish. Here are some ways to up your odds of taking them.

Pop and Swap

One of the neat ways to attract more fish to your boat for fly fishing is the popping and swapping method. It works for most inshore fish, including stripers, bluefish, sea trout, snappers and jacks. The technique is to use a large spinning outfit with a 7-inch (18-cm) popper with removed hooks. The guide or one person in the party makes a long cast and starts popping the lure back to the boat. Any fish in the area will follow the big plug, hitting it along the way. The fly anglers must be ready with a large fly rod popper ready to throw to the fish as it nears. When the fish are close enough for a short cast, fly rodders drop and start working a popper on the big plug while—on signal—the spinning angler stops the plug. You can jerk the plug out of the water, but better results have been found by leaving the floating plug in the water so that the fish transfer their interest to the working popping bug. This trick attracts fish from as large an area as can be reached with the spinning outfit and brings them to the boat.

Chumming

Chumming involves attracting fish with ground-up bait, scent or oil. Prepared chum (frozen or packaged) is available in coastal bait shops or you can make your own by grinding up local bait. If making your own, make sure to grind the chum fine—you want to attract the fish, not feed them. Some anglers and charter boats grind on the boat, while others bring along containers of ready-mixed chum. The best chumming areas are where fish are already present. Anchoring and then spreading the chum over the side. The best way to do this is to mix the chum with water to make a slurry, and then slowly but regularly ladle the mix over the side. Allow

some time for the chum slick to disperse and bring fish to the source of the chum.

Assuming right-hand casters, the best way to fly fish effectively is from the port transom corner of the cockpit. Make sure to stow outriggers or any other boat gear. Make short casts with a chum fly or short streamer into the chum slick that is mixing in the wash of the boat. Then move to the starboard side as you work the fly to allow a second fly caster to get into position to cast. Often hits will come right away, so that by the time you move out of the casting corner, you have a fish on. By doing this, you can keep up a rotation, giving all on board a chance at the chummed fish.

One of the best ways to work a shoreline is to have the guide or fishing buddy maintain a set distance away from the bank or shore so that the casting distance and line out of the rod never has to change while working that shoreline.

Saltwater fly fishing around rip rap (above) can produce a lot of different species, including stripers, blues, seatrout, perch and similar coastal species that will hang near these protected areas that also hold food and protection from strong tidal currents.

Flies have to match the bait (left) and what the fish is looking for. This big popper is an example of a fly used in saltwater fishing when using the "pop and swap" method.

Breaking Fish

Lots of saltwater fish chase baitfish to the surface. These breaking fish are pushing the bait to the top, crowding and then eating them when the baitfish can't learn to fly. Binoculars are a key to finding breaking fish on top and separating distant breaking fish from waves, boat wakes and surf pounding jetties. Birds often work over the bait and are another good indication of breaking fish.

Casting around Birds

Birds are great for signaling breaking gamefish, but they can get caught in the fly line. To avoid hook-ups with birds,

make your cast sideways or low and forceful to get in under the flock of birds working the bait. Cast short instead of long, provided that you are able to hit the breaking school. If you do see a bird diving towards a fly in the air, jerk it away from the bird immediately, since a ruined cast takes less time to recover from than untangling a hooked bird. If you see a bird that seems to be diving towards your fly or skipping bug on the surface, you have two choices as follows to prevent a bird hook-up:

- Immediately stop the fly and allow it to sink. This usually keeps a bird from following it.

- Jerk the fly or bug harder (the only choice for floating bugs) to prevent the bird from taking it. If possible, pick up the line and make a backcast to keep the bug/fly from the bird.

If you do hook a bird (everyone does eventually), reel it in so that your angling buddy can throw a towel over its head. This will quiet the bird so that one of you can hold the bird and the other untangle the line/leader from the wing or fly from the body. Release the bird gently—remember that it is not its fault that it got hooked!

Offshore Saltwater Tactics

Fly-fishing for offshore big-game species is increasingly popular; many consider it to be the last frontier of the sport. It is a three-person operation, with four people better still. It requires the angler, along with an experienced captain, mate and perhaps a second mate. The reasons become obvious.

Make sure that you are experienced with a lot of other saltwater fly fishing before attempting this, and perhaps go along on a trip with an experienced offshore fly angler just to see what is involved. A day or two as a second mate or observer goes a long way to pointing up some of the realities of the sport.

The basics of this fishing are that you are not trolling, as is done with conventional gear. Instead, you must adhere to IGFA regulations. (There is no law or regulation about this, but to date virtually all fly-fishing offshore tournaments require following IGFA guidelines in tackle, leaders, tippets, shock leaders and fishing methods.) In this, you are not casting to the fish until the boat is out of gear. It will continue to move from the inertia of the boat, but is not under control of the engines or captain. This, and the fly-casting that results to get the fly out to the fish, dictates how the boat is set up.

Tackle

The basics of tackle include a stout rod in the 12 to 15/17 line weight range, reel with several hundred yard backing capacity, shooting head of sinking line, IGFA style leader and large hackle or synthetic material fly. In addition, it helps to have special teaser rods and reels for trolling teasers and getting them in quickly when a fish is in the baits.

Fishing Boat

There are different theories, but a favored way to set up a fly fishing boat is to keep one outrigger in a stored position and troll teasers only from the other outrigger. Right-handed casters need the port rigger stored, since all casting is from the port/transom corner of the cockpit. This allows a side cast or angled cast with minimal possibility of getting tangled with the rigging of the outrigger.

Typical teaser trolling is with three conventional rods, using one as a flat line and the other two in clips at the end and middle of the outrigger. Over the years, fly anglers have tried various lengths and types of teaser rods, ranging from about 6 through 12 feet (1.8 through 3.7 m). About 9 feet (2.7 m) seems like the best choice. If you go longer than that, you have greater leverage, but it requires more strength to get in the teasers. If you go shorter, then you have the easier leverage, but lack the length to pump and reel the teasers rapidly.

Many anglers favor teaser rods where the line enters through a tunnel, to run through the center of the rod and out a special tubular tip

Big-game flies do not need to be excessively long, but they often need a popping head in front of the fly to attract and hold the attention of big-game billfish.

top. This prevents the line from flapping around in a high wind and getting caught on the guides or around the tip top. In addition, the flat line rod is fitted with a small clip release, to hold the line even lower to further prevent line bellying. High-speed reels are a must to retrieve the teaser rapidly to keep the fish interested, have the fish ready to switch to the fly and yet not able to catch the teaser or bait. Most anglers try to get as high a gear ratio as possible (short of the gears jamming or binding).

Action

With teasers all trolled from the starboard outrigger, and fly rods at the ready, the action comes when a fish appears in the baits. (This system is standard for right-hand casters; left-hand casters casting from the starboard/transom corner should store the right rigger and troll teasers from the left, or port, rigger.)

Big-water casting for stripers can be done blind casting as this angler is doing, or by searching out breaking schools of fish and casting into the school.

In these cases, the fish can appear after any one of the three teasers—long (from the tip of the outrigger), short (from the mid-point of the outrigger), and flat (the closest teaser, from the line not run trough an outrigger clip). What you do at this point depends upon which teaser the fish is after. What you don't want is the fish attracted to or switching off to any of the other baits/teasers as you reel the teaser to get the fish into the boat wash. Thus, if the fish hits the closest teaser off the flat line, you do not immediately have to reel in the other two lines, since the fish will not see them. If the fish is after the middle (short outrigger) teaser, then the mate has to immediately reel in the closest teaser (flat line rod) to prevent the fish from seeing it and switching to it. If the fish hits the long (long outrigger) teaser, then the mate and anyone else on the boat has to reel in both lines simultaneously to keep the teasers away from the fish. It also helps if the captain is experienced enough to turn the boat slightly into the teaser side to swing the teasers away from the boat during this operation.

Readying the Outfit

While all this is happening, the fly angler must ready his outfit. For this, it helps to strip enough line from the rod—usually about 30 to 40 feet (9.1 to 12.2 m). This is best stripped into a bucket in the port/transom corner to keep the line from sliding over the deck or blowing around. Flip the line into the boat wash to strip out line preparatory to casting.

Then when the captain throws the boat out of gear and the fish is in the wash, the trick is for the mate to pull the teaser from the water.

Casting and Striking

Make a sidearm or angled backcast and drop the fly in the wash on the starboard side of the boat wake. When doing this, make sure that you cast five to seven feet in back of the fish so that it turns to take the fly going away from the boat. What you don't want is a green fish taking the fly and in the process, leaping into the boat cockpit. In addition, experience shows that you cannot hook a fish coming towards you. With the fish turning, the fish is hooked somewhere in the mouth. In short, don't pull on the line as the fish starts to run from the boat. The result will be a 100-pound-plus (45.4 kg) fish breaking off. Instead, use the rod only to strike, moving the rod opposite to the direction that the fish is taking. Thus, if the fish is going to your left, strike to the right and if going to the right, strike with the rod to the left.

Fighting the Fish

As you solidly hook the fish, it will likely make a long run with some jumps in the process. When the fish jumps, some anglers "bow" to the fish, as was originated in tarpon fishing. The rationale for this might seem weak, since there is perhaps little that can be changed with the belly in the line and the fish out 100 or more yards (91.4 m). For a more detailed discussion, see Chapter 10.

Tropical Saltwater Tactics

Tropical fly fishing typically involves fishing flats or over and around reefs. It is often sight fishing, or at least fishing to structure and areas where fish are known to congregate.

Cast Away from Feeding Fish

Shallow water feeding fish such as permit, bonefish, snook, trout and others have good eyesight. Presenting a fly to them can be difficult, particularly those on an open flat such as bonefish and permit. For this, use clear or light blue (sky colored) fly lines, make your lengthening cast to the side of the fish and outside of its range of vision. Then, with a final backcast, make the final cast to the fish, dropping the fly in front of the fish by several feet so that the retrieve of the fly and the fish are on an intersecting path, with the fly seeming to flee from the fish. Make the cast so that the fly seems to be escaping from the fish, not going toward it or attacking it. Thus, the best casts are in front of the fish so that the fly can scurry away (front or side) as the fish approaches.

Retrieves for Barracuda

You can't retrieve too fast for a barracuda. In fact, too slow a retrieve will only cause the barracuda to lose interest and drift away. For a sighted barracuda, make a long cast that will put the fly in front of the fish. Begin the retrieve as the fly is falling. The retrieve must be fast, using one of the two following methods:

- Tuck the rod under your arm (left arm if a right-handed caster) and retrieve the line hand-over-hand to make the fly run straight and constantly, without the twitches and pauses of most retrieves.
- Grip the rod between your thighs and strip the line in hand-over-hand for a fast constant retrieve.

When the barracuda hits, grab the rod with your dominant hand, form a circle of your thumb and finger around the fly line to guide it as the line goes out, bow to the rod when the slack line is gone and the reel drag takes over, and fight the fish.

The teeth on some fish require wire leaders and also careful handling, as evidenced by this large barracuda taken by Brenda Pfeiffer at Costa de Cocos in Mexico.

Snook Casting

Snook fly fishing is best around mangroves, favorite haunts for these fish. For the best fishing, have the guide (or your fishing partner) pole the boat a set distance from the edges of the mangroves so that you can get a set line length for your casting. That way, you do not have to shorten or lengthen your cast each time to try to hit the edge of the mangroves. This is very important, since snook will seldom come out of the mangroves for a fly. The best that you can hope for is a snook that will dart out to the edge of the mangroves or be hanging there to take a fly when it lands.

Wading

Wading flats is vital for fishing bonefish and permit. This allows you to adjust your approach based on the path (often zigzag for bonefish) of the fish, and to get in a position to make a cast where the fly and fish will intersect. Do this safely, since stingrays inhabit the same flats waters as do bonefish and permit. For this, avoid picking your feet up and putting them down, even though this might seem easy in the shallow waters. Instead, slide your feet forward in a shuffle. This will let you to bump a stingray that will move out of the way, rather than stepping on it where it may drive a stinger into your ankle. Move very slowly in very shallow water; do not send out any water waves or rings that will scare the bonefish you are trying to reach.

Author (above) with a snook taken by working the shoreline—maintaining a set distance from the shore for easy, constant casting.

Stripers taken at night as Ed Russell has done here (right) can be a big thrill, but extreme care must be taken in casting and fish handling.

Shallow-water fishing (above left) can be done from a boat as well as wading, as the author's wife has done here to land this bonefish.

Fly fishermen can sometimes get a lot of unexpected catches (above right). This guitarfish (a relative to sharks) was taken from the surf on the West Coast near Santa Barbara.

Author (left) with a false albacore (little tunny) taken on a fly using long casts and flies to imitate the baitfish (glass minnows) in the area where the fish was feeding.

Chapter 10

Hooking, Fighting, Landing, Releasing

Releasing a trout—or any fish—successfully starts with proper handling, beginning at the moment the fish is brought to the net or the hand.

T he goal of fly fishing is to get a fish to take the fly so you can fight and land it. There is a lot to consider in this, from the take or hit to landing and releasing the fish. For simplicity, we are going to use the term "take/hit" for the fish accepting and mouthing the fly, and the term "strike" for how we react to sink the hook into the fish.

There are several ways fish hit. Blind hits occur when blind fishing an area. In this case, you feel a sudden tug or hit, in which the fish might be securely hooked or might have just mouthed the fly. If fishing a "J" hook fly, tighten up on the line until you feel the weight of the fish and then strike. If fishing a circle hook, wait until you feel the weight of the fish and let it turn to run. The hook seats itself in the corner of the mouth.

Some situations involve fishing where you have seen fish, seen surface activity that indicates fish or know that fish habitually hold in a specific area. The techniques here are little different than when blind fishing, except for a higher degree of mental readiness. The one problem that you can encounter is that by being "ready" sometimes you overreact or react and strike too quickly to a take/hit.

Similar to this is a situation with breaking fish, as often occurs in saltwater, typically with striped bass and bluefish, occasionally with largemouth bass. Use a faster retrieve than usually necessary to simulate fleeing baitfish.

Sight fishing is different in that you cast to a specific feeding-fish situation. This can be to a school or small pod of fish (such as bonefish, crappie or carp) or to an individual fish (such as trout or permit). Present the fly (this varies with species as outlined in other chapters) and be ready with the right type of strike, depending upon the position of the fish and the type of fly hook used.

Hooking Fish

Regardless of the type of take/hit and how you react, you must be prepared with your line/rod hands. This means that in all fishing—all the time—you must hold the rod securely with your rod hand and also allow the line to run through under your index finger of that rod hand. The reason for this is simple. You don't reel fly fishing gear—you strip line. To strip line, you use your line hand to pull line in and then reach forward to pull in more line. For this, do not reach ahead of your rod hand, since this requires letting go of the line (if you do not control it with your rod hand) or grab-

bing it ahead of your rod hand and then releasing line from your rod hand index finger as you continue to strip line. If you release the line and get a take/hit at that instant, you lose the fish.

In all cases, run the line under the index finger of your rod hand, and grip the line against the rod as your line hand creates slack in the line to strip. Then reach forward in back of your rod hand to grab the stripped line. This allows you to maintain a tight grip on the line at all times. If you get a take/hit any time during this retrieve, you are holding the line with your line hand or gripping the line against the rod grip with the index finger of your rod hand.

Surf fishing with a fly rod is a relatively new and demanding sport, but can be very rewarding, as this angler found out with this hook-up. Note the stripping basket strapped to his waist to keep the line from getting washed around in the surf and tangling with his feet.

During the Strike

Rod and line handling and position are important when striking, regardless of the type of fly used ("J" or circle hook). Keep the rod low during your retrieves so that you have the full power of the rod—if needed—to strike the fish.

If you are fishing in still water, keep the rod straight out toward the line. In running water, the line makes a belly. The fly—and the fish if it takes the fly—is at the end of the long arc made by the fly line bellying in the current. Point the rod towards where the fly is—or where you think it to be—and you are really creating slack in the line when a fish hits because of the angle of the rod and line. Point the rod toward the line (usually downstream of where the fish will hit) and there is no slack, even though the fish is markedly upstream from you when it hits. Often the best strike is to the side, holding the rod parallel to the water, and holding or pulling on the line as you sink the hook in the fish with the butt power of the rod.

The advantages of this method are that you can usually pull line further, quicker and more to the side to strike the fish and take up any slack or stretch than you can with an overhead strike. If you can do this with a swift pull of the line to sink the hook without moving the rod, so much the better—barring the delay that you want with circle hooks. Also, if the fish does become unbuttoned, the line will be on or in the water and the fly will not travel far—leaving the possibility that the same fish or another fish might pick up the fly.

The method of working down a river one step at a time can often yield results like this. The author is flanked by guides holding a large male Atlantic salmon taken on an imitation leech.

How you react to a hit depends upon the type of fly hook you are using. Standard or "J" hooks require an immediate reaction when you feel the weight of the fish. Circle hook flies slide to the corner of the fish's mouth as the fish turns, thus requiring a slight delay until the fish starts to fight.

HOOKING, FIGHTING, LANDING, RELEASING

There are some disadvantages to this method. If you are right-handed and strike to the right (typical) and have a tree branch, boat structure or rock to the right when a fish becomes unbuttoned, the rod can snap back, hit the obstruction and shatter. Similarly, you can hit an angling buddy standing there—or drive a fly straight towards your buddy. An alternative is to strike to the left. The reverse would apply to left-handed casters.

The overhead strike from a low rod position tends to create a time lag between the hit and the strike. You cannot or do not pull as much line on the strike, thus not striking as hard as with a side strike. You will have an advantage if you are fishing in weeds. Then, the raised rod allows lifting the line above the weeds. If a hooked fish starts a run through weeds, a low rod position on the strike drags the line through the weeds and can allow the fish to break off from the increased pressure on the tippet. The disadvantage is that an overhead strike tends to pull a fish to the surface where it can jump free.

The above basically describes a strip-strike, or a combination of a strip-strike and rod strike. The basics for this are pulling the line from in back of the index finger of the rod hand, to strip in line to sink the hook in the fish. These are used with "normal" tippet tests that will not break under the strip-strike method. Usually, you are safe with this strike method with about 4-pound test (1.8-kg) and heavier tippets.

Use slip strikes with light tippets in the 4-pound (1.8-kg) test or lighter, or by those who break off fish with heavier tippets. This is best with small flies and light tippets when casting to wary fish. This generally applies to tippets in the 3X through 8X category.

To make a slip-strike, move the rod to the side, while releasing the grip on the line to allow the line to slip through the guides. Done right, this creates a gentle pressure on the hook to sink the point, while not creating enough force to snap the fine tippet.

If dealing with big fish or fish with hard mouths (such as tarpon), strike several times. Grip the line, then rapidly and forcefully lever the rod to the side several times to sink the hook in the fish. Note that you can do this with "J" hooks as soon as the fish hits, but you must wait until the fish turns with circle hooks. If a fish is running, this also requires allowing the line to slip grudgingly through your line hand while making the strike, retaining enough force in the rod strike to sink the hook.

Fish Reaction to Strikes

Once you strike the fish, the fish makes the next decision for you. If it is a small fish, strip it in—even though it fights, runs to the side, jumps, thrashes around or otherwise objects. Larger fish usually run. This may be a short run— you may have to do little more than lower the rod for the few feet that the fish moves or allow a few feet of line to flow through the guides.

In the case of a large/strong fish, it usually makes an immediate long run. For this, clear the stripped line through the guides. This means that the line must not have any knots, loops or tangles that might catch in a guide. If wading, the surface tension of the water helps to hold the line untangled to easily flow through the guides.

A caution here—if you are using a wading staff, have a net dangling in the water, wear hip boots with straps or are fishing in weeds or around structure, the line may tangle. For this, the best line-handling solution is to strip in very large coils of line as you retrieve and hold each coil with a different finger of your line hand so that you can release them smoothly and easily as a fish runs. If you need more than four coils (you will on most retrieves) use a slightly smaller coil on the second four coils so that the coils flow out during a cast without tangling.

If fishing from a boat, stow all tackle before casting so that you have a completely clean deck on which to strip line. Alternatively, throw a 6-foot-square (1.8-m) net over the tackle so that the line can't tangle with other gear. Hold the rod high and allow the line to flow through a circle made with the index finger and thumb of your line hand. Once the last of the line clears through this finger/thumb ring, the reel drag takes over. At this time, drop the rod slightly and push the rod towards the fish to lessen the shock of the switch from an almost-free flow of line to the resistance of the reel drag.

Fighting Fish

To fight fish, the rod is a flexible lever that serves as a leaf spring to prevent breakoffs. There are several good strategies to help you be successful. Here are a few:

Using Side Pressure

Realize that the 30/60-degree angle of a rod does not require that the rod stay in a vertical plane. You can hold the rod at any angle above horizontal. For horizontal fishfighting, hold the rod parallel

To fight fish, the best angle for the rod is between about 30 and 60 degrees, as shown by Joe Zimmer. This maximizes the shock absorbency of the rod to prevent line breakage and also minimizes the possibility of rod breakage.

HOOKING, FIGHTING, LANDING, RELEASING

30/60 Degree Angle

The lower the rod is angled (below about 30 degrees from horizontal), the less shock absorbency you have. The higher you hold a rod (beyond about 60 degrees from horizontal), the more danger to the rod without any real gain in shock absorbency. So, for the most part, keep the rod angle between 30 and 60 degrees.

There are, however, exceptions to the 30/60 rule:

- If a fish is in weeds. Here, use a high rod—perhaps with the butt 90 degrees to the horizontal—to hold the line high and minimize excessive weed drag that can break off a fish. Stand instead of sit and hold the rod high (over your head) to maximize elevation of the rod and line.
- If fishing stickups, hold the rod high and above the stickup to clear the line, even in open waters. This is typical of flats water with mangrove stubs, but can also occur anywhere. It is most effective where the stubs or stickups are short—such as with emergent mangrove seedlings. It is least effective (but sometimes the only choice possible) with high stickups that may not be possible to clear with the line.
- The same situation and reasoning can apply to other low structure such as rocks, logs, coral heads, lobster or crab floats. For all of these, raise the rod high to clear the object.
- The high rod also reduces the amount of the fly line in the water, thus reducing the pressure of dragging the line. The pressure of just dragging the line through the water increases with the size (weight) of the line and the speed of the fish. Often, you do not even need a reel drag setting for this situation, since the pressure of pulling the line is enough drag on the fish. With light tackle in particular and light tippets, raising the rod while maintaining a light reel drag may prevent a break-off.
- Angle the rod to one side to keep the line away from surface structure. Doing this can prevent or minimize abrasion of the line when a fish runs around structure. Examples would be a bass running around a stump or a trout running around a rock.
- Use a high rod tactic with little drag if a fish runs past structure that you are trying to clear. Loosen the drag if necessary, but tighten it again when the fish reaches open water. This allows you to coax the fish into open water where you can fight it easily.
- Another exception to the 30/60 rule is when a big fish runs and you are rapidly approaching the end of the line and beginning of the backing. Regardless of the type of connection that you have between line and backing, a high rod angle increases the possibility of line/backing connections catching in guides. As the end of the line approaches, drop the rod to horizontal to eliminate the angle between the rod guides and allow the connection to flow freely through the guides.
- Use the same horizontal rod technique when reeling in the backing/line connection to reduce any guide hang-up. This is easy to do during the "lowered rod" stage of pumping the fish as you reel to gain line and before raising the rod again.
- Drop the rod straight down when a fish dives under the boat. Boat-hooked fish can run under the boat, going to the opposite side. To stop this from happening, stick the rod straight down into the water. Watch the tip if you are fishing shallows. Check that the line and leader clears the boat hull. You may have to move to the bow or stern, still with the rod tip underwater, to get to the opposite side of the boat and continue the fight.

Here, Joe Zimmer shows the action of holding the rod to the side to turn a fish (Atlantic salmon) to get it in close for landing. This action often turns a fish that would be impossible to turn otherwise.

to the water, only about a foot (30.5 cm) above the water surface if wading, and maintain the 30/60-degree angle of the rod with the fish.

The rationale for doing this, in contrast to the high rod situations above, is that it allows you to turn the head of a fish to the side more easily. It is also a good technique to switch to from the overhead vertical rod position. Let's take a fish running away from you.

The fish is in a straight line with the leader and pulling in the same way that an unruly dog on a leash would pull along its owner. Switch that leash angle to the side, and the dog is pulled to the side to lose the direct pull strength it had when forging ahead.

The same occurs with fish. By rapidly going to a side angle from an overhead angle, you can pull a fish to the side where you can control it—

pulling its head and making it fight the way you want, not the way it wants. Even though the fish now has its broad body to help fight you, it might swim at right angles to the line, rather than pulling away from it. With big fish or long-running fish, you often have to use both the high rod and horizontal rod angles. Use the high rod to allow the fish to make the first long, sustained run, and then switch to the side angle to fight the fish, turn its head and work it close for landing. With big fish, there can be multiple runs so that you may have to switch rod angles back and forth several times.

Pumping

You fight fish by pumping with the rod. This allows you to fight and land fish that in weight are far in excess of the tippet strength used. You can do this with the rod in any plane. Let's look at this from a vertical plane. Once a fish has slowed and then stopped from a long run, reel in line as you lower the rod (angle it straight towards the line) until you feel the pressure from the fish. Do not just drop the rod and then reel in line, as this can tangle the line around the rod tip. Grip the reel by the palming plate/rim and raise the rod. By raising the rod, you are using a lever (albeit a flexible one) to gain line. Then repeat, but lower the rod as you reel in line. At any time during this continuous process you can release line to allow a fish to run.

With all pumping, maintain

constant even pressure on the fish. This means that you must try to equal the pressure that you create while raising the rod each time that you do this. When reeling in line, you are not really creating pressure on the fish, but only retrieving line that you gained by levering the rod up to gain line.

Level Wind the Reel

Fly fishing reels do not have a level wind. When reeling in line/backing to load a reel, as well as reeling in line when fighting a fish, you must level wind the line manually. Do this with your little finger of your rod hand, using it as a guide to spool the line back and forth on the spool. Usually this is done when you are pumping, dropping the rod down as you reel line. Make sure that you keep the line tight on the reel to prevent loose line from digging into previous line wraps.

Watch out for line cuts when a fish is running. Keep your fingers away from the reel (because of the spinning handle of direct-drive reels). Fly line does not cause much damage, but you can get cut from backing, particularly with the new, thin gel-spun lines.

Loosen Drag

On long runs of fish, it is best to reduce the drag. The drag from the line as a big fish runs is often enough drag, and the addition of a reel drag will only increase the possibility of too much pressure on the outfit and the tippet snapping. This advice comes with a big "if." The "if" is if you can later reset the drag to the

original setting. Check this by pulling line from the reel to get a rough idea of the drag setting. Then loosen the drag so that there is little pressure on backing flowing from the reel. This is easy if you have a lever drag fly reel, since you can easily note the spot where the lever was set, back it off, and then reset it later to the same spot. If you have a knob operated drag, count the number of turns or partial turns/twists (or clicks, if it has a audible detent system) that you make with your hand, free the line and then later make the same number of opposite twists/ turns to reset the drag. Once you have reset the drag, check it by pulling line from the reel. The only danger with this system is that if you reset the drag to a higher setting, you again risk snapping the tippet later in the fight. If you forget to reset it, you might lose the fish when you try to land it.

Push Rod to Fish

On long runs, the standard procedure for tarpon anglers is to push the rod to the fish to lessen any line pressure from six feet of thrashing gills, fins and scales. In doing this, you don't reduce as much pressure on the fish as you think, since the line is still dragging in the water. You do reduce the risk of the tippet being snapped by the thrashing fish. You can also do this with other large fish that are jumpers, notably salmon (Atlantic and Pacific), pike, musky, large bass, dolphin and snook.

Landing Fish

There are lots of ways to land fish, with the most common being by hand. Often this involves lipping the fish and is typically used with smallmouth and largemouth bass, stripers, redfish, small tarpon and such. Do this only on fish that do not have teeth, lack crushers in the throat and cannot harm you. It can't be done with small-mouthed fish such as panfish, most trout and carp. Since fly fishing involves single hook flies (most of the time) it is relatively safe. (One danger is when using a tandem fly rig or when fishing a second fly off of a dropper. In situations like this, the thrashing fish might flip free and imbed the second fly or hook into you.)

To lip a fish, lead the fish to you, and note where the fly is located in its mouth. If possible, try to grab the fish by the mouth opposite the fly location. Stick your thumb in the fish's mouth, then clamp against your index finger and lift. Note that a firm grip is a must, particularly with fish over a few pounds, which can be incredibly strong. Unless it is a very small fish, use your other hand to support the fish by the belly as you lift it to reduce damage to its jaw.

For small broad fish such as sunfish, grasp around the fish, using your finger and thumb to depress the spines in the dorsal and pectoral fins. Grab trout and bonefish the same way, using your index and middle finger on each side of one pectoral fin to keep the fish from slipping from your grasp.

Gloves and Towels

Cotton gloves and towels provide a firmer grip to help hand-land fish. It might seem that gloves (like simple cotton work gloves) are best, but they are a nuisance to wear all the time and difficult to put on when wet. Plus, it is impossible to tie knots while wearing gloves. The best solution is a small wet towel that you can grab with your hand and slip around a fish or into a fish's mouth. Allow the towel to touch only the fish's mouth if you plan to release the fish, since body contact will remove the fish's slime.

Hook Release

Over the years, anglers have discovered and developed special tools for releasing hooks from fish. Here are a few good ones to have:

- Pronged hook disgorger— Use standard forked-end disgorgers mostly for panfish. They push the hook back to unhook the panfish and work it out of the mouth. These are designed for removal of bare hooks and do not work well on panfish and sunfish to remove poppers or sliders, which will fill up the mouth and make it impossible to get the disgorger into the fish. They do work for removal of streamers and wet flies.
- Hemostat—Hemostats are basic tools for fly removal. I like the straight jaw tools better than the curved jaw hemostats, since they make it easier to get a firm grip on the fly. Grind or file down the teeth on these, since the heavy teeth often twist or damage small fly hooks. To use, grip the fly hook by the bend to prevent fly damage and push back. If you can keep the hemostat almost parallel with the plane of the fly hook, it is easier to push the fly back to unhook the fish. Better are the Dr. Slick Side-Cutter Clamps that have smaller serrations on one jaw and a flat surface on the other jaw for gentler gripping.
- Ketchum releaser—These handled tools have a small tube, open on one side to slip over the leader and slid down to the fly to push the fly back and out of the fish. Different sizes are made for freshwater and saltwater fly fishing. They work great.
- "J" shaped release tool—This simple device requires lifting the fish (you must have a

To lip fish by hand (far left), a wet towel makes it easy to grab the fish and prevent losing it. The wet towel also eliminates the need to grab the fish elsewhere and makes it easy to remove the fly hook while holding the fish and then to release it carefully into the water with minimal handling.

Use a towel or net over the front motor controls (left) to continue using the controls without them tangling up the fly line when it is stripped onto the deck.

heavy enough leader), then grabbing the fly by the bend with the "J" tool. To release the fish, pull down on the leader and up on the "J" tool so that the fly point is straight down to pop the fish off of the fly. Use them for toothy critters, such as bluefish, to avoid handling.

- "Q" shaped release tool— These handled tools are similar to the "J" tool, but end in a corkscrew or pig tail "Q"-shaped end to slip over the line and slide down to the fly. Use the "Q" end to push against the fly bend and release the fly.

- Pliers—Long-nose pliers allow grabbing the bend of the hook and forcibly pushing back on the hook to remove it. In addition, pliers have many other fishing uses.
- Catch-and-release "pliers"— These grippers are made with one or both jaws in an arc to grab the fish by the lower jaw, yet avoid crushing the lip area. They make it easy to hold the fish so that you can use one of the above tools (or your fingers, if the fish does not have teeth) to remove the fly.
- Gripper—Special grippers that began with the Boga

Grip and have since spawned a lot of imitators are open jaw grippers that allow easy opening to grip a fish's lower jaw. Some, like the Boga grip, also weigh the fish. These are handy, but do not use them on very large fish, which cannot support all their weight from their lower jaw. You can grab large fish with a Boga grip, but support the fish with a hand under its belly.

Fish Net

Net fish head first, as is being done with this large striper. That way, if the fish dives from contact with the net frame, it will dive into the net rather than out of the net as would occur were it netted tail first.

Using a net to hold and stabilize a fish is a great way to keep a fish calm while removing a fly preparatory to release. Here, Capt. Norm Bartlett (foreground) holds and unhooks the fish caught by Newell Steele (background).

The basics of landing fish remain the same. First, if you are netting the fish yourself, make sure that you know how to do it. If a fishing partner is landing the fish, make sure that he or she is experienced. Make sure that the fish is tired enough to land safely.

Place the net in the water before the fish comes into view. If you do this in front of the fish it may frighten it into thrashing or making another run. If fishing in a current (tide or river current) place the net down-current of the fish so that the net blossoms out to capture the fish, rather than being pushed back out of the net rim.

Lead the fish into the net head first. If the net and fish touch, the fish will dive head first into the net. If you net tail first, any fish/net contact will spook the fish out of the net. With the fish in the net, slack off on the line pressure and immediately raise the net and fish. If the net is deep, turn the net frame sideways to contain the fish and eliminate the possibility of it jumping out.

Even if you do not plan to keep the fish or to remove it from the net for a hero photo shot, the net tends to stabilize the fish while you remove the hook. This is best handled with a partner—one of you to hold the net containing the fish while the other removes the hook. An exception to the above is to keep the fish and net in the water while carefully removing the hook and then releasing the fish.

HOOKING, FIGHTING, LANDING, RELEASING

Lip Gaff

Realize that hand gaffs, as with any gaff, are potentially dangerous. Hand gaff a fish through the lower lip to stabilize it while removing the hook, and you can still release it unharmed. There are two ways to do this. One is to control the fish until you can reach it easily with the hand gaff, then bring the gaff up under the lower jaw and raise the gaff rapidly to hook the fish. Keep the fish in the water to remove the fly. To lift the fish would injure it with its weight hanging from its lower jaw. An alternative is to carefully place the gaff into the fish's mouth, then stab down through the floor of the mouth. This allows pinning the gaff to the underside of the boat gunwale to stabilize the fish for fly removal.

Use a standard gaff (hand or long-handled) to gaff a "keep" fish. Reach over the fish with the gaff and gaff it up through the body just a little in back of the shoulders. Hitting the fish in back of the shoulders tends to equalize the weight of the front and back of the fish on the gaff and make it easier to get the fish into the boat.

Landing Fish from a Boat

Land a fish from a boat by hand, net, gaff or with a gripper (Boga Grip or similar tools). For this, make absolutely sure that you do not have anything (small camera or cell phone, in particular) in your breast shirt pocket. They can fall out or get damaged. If there are waves, try to land the fish on the lee side to minimize problems. Lead the fish to the boat. Follow the directions above for details on using each type of landing method. In the case of fish that you are netting to remove the hook to release the fish, use

From a drift boat while fishing the James River, Blane Chocklett caught this smallmouth on a fly rod.

King Montgomery reaches for a net to land his fly-rod-caught crappie. Hand landing small fish such as this is also an option.

One easy way to land fish and handle them while weighing them at the same time is with a Boga grip or similar fish-grabbing device that allows lipping the fish without danger to the angler if the fish has teeth. This false albacore (little tunny) would not be a danger, but the gripping tool still makes handling and releasing easy.

the net only to contain the fish. This is also best with lip hand gaffing methods. Keep the fish in the water to reduce stress and increase its chances of survival. If you are netting or gaffing to keep the fish, immediately bring it into the boat and into a ready iced fish box where you can remove the fly and resume fishing.

Landing Fish from Shore

If you are landing a fish while shore fishing, how you react depends upon whether you are keeping or releasing the fish. If you are keeping the fish, work the fish into the shallows until you beach it, where you can net or gaff it. You can also keep fish on a stringer or in a holding net (small fish only).

If wade fishing, be cautious about keeping fish or using a stringer if sharks are around. You don't want to be tied to a chum line for feeding sharks. To release a fish, do not let it touch the bottom, since this can remove the protective slime and reduce chances of survival. Keep it in deep enough water to allow it to swim while removing the hook.

Landing Fish on a Beach

When landing fish from a beach, you can use the same techniques as when landing fish from the shore, with the added advantage of waves. Use the wave action to swim the fish into the shore with each wave that will push the tired fish closer to the beach. (This is not

100 percent—some shorelines are steep, with little wave action or have troughs next to the beach which prevent this.) Then handle the fish as with shore landing methods.

Landing Fish while Wading

Netting is the safest way to land fish when wading. Follow directions as above. Most anglers just use their hands to land fish. The best way to land fish while wading depends upon the fish. Hand landing is often best with fish like smallmouth and largemouth bass lip landed. Lift trout by the body just in back of the pectoral fins. Catfish have spines, which require grabbing the fish over the body in back of the dorsal spine and around the

HOOKING, FIGHTING, LANDING, RELEASING

pectoral spines. It often helps to hold trout belly up, since this tends to quiet or temporarily paralyze them. Holding a fish by the lip or turned over as with trout also makes removing the fly easy.

Landing Fish on Flats

Handle fish caught on flats (like bonefish, permit, redfish and sea trout) just as you would any catch taken from a boat or while wading. Net, hand land or gaff the fish when boat fishing, or grip the fish by hand or with a Boga type of tool. Remove the hook and release the fish or immediately store it on ice if keeping it.

Releasing Fish

Many of us today release fish, although there is nothing wrong with keeping a fish or two for the table. David Woronecki, a retired fisheries biologist with the Maryland Department of Natural Resources, believes that the angler's attitude toward fish during its capture and release is vital to their survival. "The person handling the fish during its release is the most important factor relative to the well-being and ultimate survival of the fish," he states. He also likes the benefits of circle hooks (now available for fly tying) and

also likes the idea—more prevalent in bait than fly fishing—of cutting the leader as close as possible to the hook to give deeply hooked fish the best chance of survival.

He also believes in careful and proper handling, as above. "I hate what I see so often on the TV fishing shows. Anglers should be subjected to the same 'holds' as they give to the fish and should be kept underwater the same length of time they keep a fish out of the water." Of course, most of what he is talking about on TV involves hardware fishing, but the same concerns apply to fly anglers.

Nine Best Methods for Releasing Fish:

1. Don't fight the fish to a point of exhaustion (its, not yours), but also make sure that it is not "green" or fresh where it could injure you or itself.
2. If the fish is big or toothy, it helps to have a knowledgeable partner assist as you land and release it.
3. Keep the fish in the water as much as possible to minimize stress.
4. Remove the fly from the fish using the methods and tools described above.

5. Hold the fish gently, preferably by the mouth—unless teeth prevent this.
6. Move the fish back and forth in the water to wash water over the gills. Or hold the fish facing into the current so that water flows over the gills.
7. Continue this until the fish recovers and makes a positive move to escape.
8. To release smaller fish (up to several pounds) hold the fish under the belly as you work it back and forth or support it in the current.

9. Never release a fish until it is ready to "escape" from you, and tries actively to do so. Releasing an exhausted fish often results in its dying from a lack of ability to pump water over its gills, or through post-release predation from sharks and barracuda.

Afterword

Large streams are often best fished early in the morning, particularly around shallows. Often fish will cruise these shallow areas early and late where they are more easily taken on flies, particularly surface or shallow-water patterns.

Fishing Conservation, Some Final Thoughts

I started fishing almost 60 years ago and have been fly fishing and tying flies for a little over 50 years. During that time a lot has occurred that has made all fishing both easier and harder. That applies especially to fly fishing. The easy parts are often pretty obvious. We have obviously developed more and better tackle. In fifty years of fly fishing we have gone from bamboo and the early, post-WWII soft whippy hollow fiberglass rods to those of graphite, with advanced progressive tapers, better ferruling systems, improved guides, high tech reel seats, better designs and actions.

With the self-ferruling system of today we no longer have to deal with the metal ferrules that add weight, reduce action, decrease sensitivity and do nothing positive other than allowing the rod to be dismantled and stored. Today we have three- four- and five-piece rods (sometimes even more sections) that make travel and storage easier and fishing no less efficient and pleasurable. Stronger and better guides, improved reel seats and advanced epoxies to coat the nylon wraps make for tough, durable, pleasant-to-fish rods.

Reels too have gone from those with assembled parts to reels with machined frames and spools, better drags of several different designs, hard anodizing for weather and salt protection, and greater line capacity. Lines have progressed from the braided and early coated lines of fifty years ago when the debate was hot and heavy over the relative merits of silk lines vs. that unproven new upstart, nylon. Since then, coating methods have allowed making better floating lines, faster-sinking lines, sinking tip lines of a variety of styles and lines geared to specific conditions (tropical, cold weather lines, big fly, long cast, etc.), and fish (bonefish, tarpon, bass and trout), all in colors to rival the NBC peacock.

There are better materials for waders, more user-friendly fishing vests, telescoping wading staffs, stripping baskets for boat and stream, improved fly boxes, better tools and new materials for fly tying, boats specifically designed for fly fishing, and gadgets galore for all types of fishing and fly fishing. Fly fishermen no longer use silk leaders nor have to soak them in water before use.

Flies have benefited also with the development of new materials, with more and more synthetics replacing the standard materials of the past. These synthetics in flies are great and have brought about a resurgence of interest in fly fishing. But tragically, much of this replacement is caused by the fact that many of the birds and animals formerly commonly used for fly tying are now on rare, threatened or endangered species lists throughout the world and no are longer legal to import into this country.

This also points out the bad of fishing and fly fishing. When I started fishing a half century ago, there were approximately 150 million people in this country. Today, we have 300 million, with the population continuing to increase through both birth rate and immigration (legal and illegal). But they aren't making any more real estate, there are no more rivers or streams and any added lakes are man-made and at the expense of those fishing streams/rivers that are dammed and flooded. We have no more fishing water today than our grand-daddies—or great grand-daddies—had a bunch of decades ago. In fact, we have far less, with recent reports indicating that up to 40 percent of the waters in this country are unsuitable for drinking, swimming and fishing. That means that we have lost over a third of the water that we might otherwise have for fishing, but which is now too polluted to hold fish, or too polluted for us to safely wade or boat and risk exposure to.

The result is that we often have twice—or more—as many fishermen on any given body of water, with fewer bodies of water on which to fish. The result is congestion on the streams, rivers, creeks, bays, and oceans, along with more congestion on the roads that take you from home to fishing spot, and more trash and waste threatening our waterways. We have too many people, period, and no one wants to consider or deal with this elephant in the living room.

The good of this otherwise dismal picture is an increased awareness of the environment, the necessity of protecting it, and the value of healthy waterways for fishing and drinking. But it also points out problems that are far greater than figuring out the best trout water, getting the latest super fly line, or tying the killer saltwater fly.

There are groups that are tying to do something about this—including not only conservation and environmental groups of all stripes, but also fishing groups such as:

Trout Unlimited (800-834-2419 www.tu.org), Federation of Fly Fishers (406-585-7592 www.fedflyfishers.org) and Coastal Conservation Association (800-201-3474 www.joincca.org).

There is also an increasing awareness that we don't have to keep every fish we take. There is nothing wrong with keeping fish for a meal or two, but the past waste and strings of fish filling a photo as "proof" of fishing prowess and "manly skill" are fortunately relics of the past. The magazines and TV shows have also echoed this, the former never showing strings of fish anymore and the latter fostering the attitude of "catch-and-release."

The philosophy of catch and release is good and as Lee Wulff said, "A fish is too valuable to be caught only once." It went from the salmon and trout camps of Lee to the bass fishing tournaments as popularized by the Bass Anglers Sportsman Society, to the offshore marlin fishing where surveys show that 90 percent or more of billfish are released by recreational anglers.

The answer to better fishing—better fly fishing—is a better planet that includes cleaner water, fewer toxins, cleaner air, less use and misuse of natural resources, more concern for the future and for the future of our children.

The bottom line for all of this is that we just have too many people in the world today, and that we are using resources faster than we can replace them—when we can replace them—and many we can't. The answer is for conservation organizations—as well as other organizations, governments, agencies and groups—to start promoting, paying for and advocating more vasectomies and more condoms. We need a smaller world, a gentler world, a quieter world, a caring world.

Further Reading

Bates, Joseph, D. Jr. *Streamer Fly Tying And Fishing,* Mechanicsburg, PA, Stackpole Books, 1966, 368 pages.

Borger, Gary. *Presentation,* Wausau, WI, Tomorrow River Press, 1995, 319 pages.

Budworth, Geoffrey. *The Complete Book of Fishing Knots,* New York, NY, The Lyons Press, 1999, 144 pages.

Combs, Trey. *Bluewater Fly Fishing,* New York, NY, Lyons & Burford, 1995, 285 pages.

Connett, Eugene V. *My Friend the Trout,* Princeton, NJ, D. Van Nostrand Company, Inc. 1961, 117 pages.

Earnhardt, Tom. *Fly fishing Tidewaters,* New York, NY, Lyons & Burford, 1995, 179 pages.

Gierach, John. *Fly Fishing Small Streams,* Mechanicsburg, PA, Stackpole Books, 1989, 159 pages.

Hauptman, Cliff. *The Fly Fisher's Guide to Warmwater Lakes,* New York, NY, Lyons & Burford, 1995 168 pages.

Hughes, Dave. *Reading the Water,* Mechanicsburg, PA, Stackpole Books, 1988, 223 pages.

Humphreys, Joe. *Joe Humphreys's Trout Tactics,* Mechanicsburg, PA, Stackpole Books, 1981, 256 pages.

Humphreys, Joe. *On the Trout Stream with Joe Humphreys,* Mechanicsburg, PA, Stackpole Books, 1989, 228 pages.

Jaworowski, Ed. *The Cast,* Mechanicsburg, PA, Stackpole Books, 1992, 222 pages.

Johnson, Paul C. *The Scientific Angler,* New York, NY, Charles Scribner's Sons, 1984, 289 pages.

Kageyama, Colin J. O.D., F.C.O.V.D. *What Fish See: Understanding Optics and Color Shifts for Designing Lures and Flies,* Portland, OR, Frank Amato Publications, Inc., 1999, 183 pages.

Koch, Ed. *Fishing the Midge,* Rockville Center, NY, Freshet Press, 1972, 158 pages.

—. *Terrestrial Fishing,* Mechanicsburg, PA, Stackpole Books, 1990, 173 pages.

Kreh. Lefty. *Lefty Kreh's Ultimate Guide to Fly Fishing,* New York, NY, The Lyons Press, 2003, 405 pages.

—. *Advanced Fly-Fishing Techniques,* New York, NY, The Lyons Press, 2002, 248 pages.

—. *Presenting The Fly,* New York, NY, The Lyons Press, 1999, 352 pages.

—. *Fly Fishing in Salt Water,* New York, NY, The Lyons Press, 1997, 321 pages.

—. *Fly Casting With Lefty Kreh,* Philadelphia, PA, J. B. Lippincott Company, 1974, 127 pages.

—. *Longer Fly Casting,* New York, NY, Lyons & Burford, 191, 101 pages.

—. *Saltwater Fly-Casting Techniques,* New York, NY, The Lyons Press, 2002, 82 pages.

—. *Solving Fly-Casting Problems,* New York, NY, The Lyons Press, 2000, 90 pages.

Kumiski, Capt. John. *Saltwater Fly Fishing,* Point Pleasant, NJ, The Fisherman Library Corp., 1994, 198 pages.

Marinaro, Vincent C. *A Modern Dry Fly Code,* New York, NY, G. P. Putnam's Sons, 1950, 269 pages.

Meck, Charles R. *The Hatches Made Simple,* Woodstock, VT, The Countryman Press, 2002, 261 pages.

Meck, Charles. *Patterns, Hatches, Tactics And Trout,* Williamsport, PA, Vivid Publishing, 1995, 338 pages.

Meck, Charles. *Fishing Small Streams With A Fly Rod,* Woodstock, VT, The Countryman Press, 1991, 196 pages.

Migdalski, Ed. *The Inquisitive Angler,* New York, NY, Lyons and Burford, 1991, 221 pages.

Mitchell, Ed. *Fly Rodding the Coast,* Mechanicsburg, PA, Stackpole Books, 1995, 322 pages.

Murray, Harry. *Fly Fishing for Smallmouth Bass,* New York, NY, The Lyons Press, 1989, 190 pages.

Notley, Larry V. *Fly Leaders & Knots,* Portland, OR, Frank Amato Publications, Inc., 1998, 64 pages.

Owen, Peter. *The Field & Stream Fishing Knots Handbook,* New York, NY, The Lyons Press, 1999, 107 pages.

Pfeiffer, C. Boyd. *The Complete Photo Guide to Fly Fishing,* Minnetonka, MN, Creative Publishing, international, Inc. 2005, 127 pages

—. *Simple Flies,* Woodstock, VT, The Countryman Press, 2005, 178 pages.

—. *Fly Fishing—Bass Basics,* Mechanicsburg, PA, Stackpole Books, 1997, 168 pages.

—. *Fly Fishing—Saltwater Basics,* Mechanicsburg, PA, Stackpole Books, 1999, 232 pages.

—. *Shad Fishing,* Mechanicsburg, PA, Stackpole Books, 2002, 226 pages.

—. *Tying Trout Flies,* Iola, WI, Krause Publishing, 2002, 160 pages.

—. *Tying Warmwater Flies,* Iola, WI, Krause Publishing, 2003, 160 pages.

—. *Bug Making,* New York, NY, Lyons & Burford, 1993, 271 pages.

Reynolds, Barry and Berryman, John. *Pike on the Fly,* Boulder, CO, Johnson Books, 1993, 166 pages.

Reynolds, Barry, Befus, Brad and Berryman, John. *Carp on the Fly,* Boulder, CO, Johnson Books, 1997, 155 pages.

Reynolds, John. *Flyfishing for Sailfish,* Machynlleth, Wales, Coch-Y-Bonddu Books, 1997, 80 pages.

Samson, Jack. *Permit on a Fly,* Mechanicsburg, PA, Stackpole Books, 1996, 202 pages.

—. *Billfish on a Fly,* Portland OR, Frank Amato Publications, Inc., 1995, 80 pages.

Schwiebert, Ernest G. Jr. *Matching the Hatch,* New York, NY, The Macmillan Company, 1955, 211 pages.

— *Trout,* (two volumes) New York, NY, E. P. Dutton, Inc., 1984, 1834 pages.

Sosin, Mark and Clark, John. *Through the Fish's Eye,* New York, NY, Harper & Row, 1973, 249 pages.

Sosin, Mark and Kreh, Lefty. *Practical Fishing Knots, II,* New York, NY, Lyons & Burford, 1991, 139 pages.

Tabory, Lou. *Inshore Fly Fishing,* New York, NY, The Lyons Press, 1992, 312 pages.

Tapply, William G. *Bass Bug Fishing,* New York, NY, The Lyons Press, 1999, 142 pages.

Whitlock, Dave. *L. L. Bean Fly Fishing For Bass Handbook,* New York, NY, The Lyons Press, 1988, 157 pages.

Wilson, Terry and Wilson, Roxanne. *Bluegill Fly Fishing & Flies,* Portland, OR, Frank Amato Publications, Inc., 1999, 151 pages.

Wright, Leonard M. *The Field & Stream Fish Finding Handbook,* New York, NY, The Lyons Press, 1999, 120 pages.

Wulff, Joan. *Joan Wulff's Fly Casting Techniques,* New York, NY, Nick Lyons Books, 1987, 243 pages.

Index

Creative Publishing international
Your Complete Source of How-to Information for the Outdoors

Hunting Books
- Advanced Turkey Hunting
- Advanced Whitetail Hunting
- Bowhunting Equipment & Skills
- Bowhunter's Guide to Accurate Shooting
- The Complete Guide to Hunting
- Dog Training
- Elk Hunting
- How to Think Like a Survivor
- Hunting Record-Book Bucks
- Mule Deer Hunting
- Muzzleloading
- Outdoor Guide to Using Your GPS
- Pronghorn Hunting
- Waterfowl Hunting
- Whitetail Hunting
- Whitetail Techniques & Tactics
- Wild Turkey

Fishing Books
- Advanced Bass Fishing
- The Art of Freshwater Fishing
- Catching Panfish
- The Complete Guide to Freshwater Fishing

- Fishing for Catfish
- Fishing Rivers & Streams
- Fishing Tips & Tricks
- Fishing with Artificial Lures
- Inshore Salt Water Fishing
- Kids Gone Campin'
- Kids Gone Fishin'
- Largemouth Bass
- Live Bait Fishing
- Modern Methods of Ice Fishing
- Northern Pike & Muskie
- Offshore Salt Water Fishing
- Salt Water Fishing Tactics
- Smallmouth Bass
- Striped Bass Fishing: Salt Water Strategies
- Successful Walleye Fishing
- Trout
- Ultralight Fishing

Fly Fishing Books
- Advanced Fly Fishing
- The Art of Fly Tying
- The Art of Fly Tying – CD ROM
- Complete Photo Guide to Fly Fishing

- Complete Photo Guide to Fly Tying
- Fishing Dry Flies
- Fishing Nymphs, Wet Flies & Streamers
- Fly-Fishing Equipment & Skills
- Fly Fishing for Beginners
- Fly Fishing for Trout in Streams
- Fly-Tying Techniques & Patterns

Cookbooks
- All-Time Favorite Game Bird Recipes
- America's Favorite Fish Recipes
- America's Favorite Wild Game Recipes
- Babe & Kris Winkelman's Great Fish & Game Recipes
- Backyard Grilling
- Cooking Wild in Kate's Camp
- Cooking Wild in Kate's Kitchen
- Dressing & Cooking Wild Game
- The New Cleaning & Cooking Fish
- Preparing Fish & Wild Game
- The Saltwater Cookbook
- Slow Cookers Go Wild!
- Venison Cookery

To purchase these or other Creative Publishing international titles,
contact your local bookseller, or visit our website at
www.creativepub.com

The Freshwater Angler™   THE COMPLETE **HUNTER**™   *The Complete* FLY FISHERMAN™